D1050608

Competency Based Human Resource Management

Competency Based Human Resource Management

Value-Driven Strategies for Recruitment, Development and Reward

— Edited by —
Alain Mitrani
Murray Dalziel
— and —
David Fitt

HayGroup

Kogan Page is the UK member of the Euro Business Publishing Network.
The European members are: Les Editions d'Organisation, France; Verlag Moderne Industrie, Germany; Almqvist & Wiksell, Sweden; Franco Angeli, Italy; and Deusto, Spain. The Network has been established in response to the growing demand for international business information and to make the work of Network authors available in other European languages.

First published in French as *Des Compétences et des Hommes* in 1992 by Les Editions d'Organisation, Paris

This edition published in 1992
Reprinted 1992, 1993 (twice)

Kogan Page Limited
120 Pentonville Road
London N1 9JN

ISBN 2-7081-1515-4

British Library Cataloguing in Publication Data

A CIP record for this book is available from the British Library.

ISBN 0 7494 0771 9

Typeset by DP Photosetting, Aylesbury, Bucks
Printed and bound in Great Britain by
Biddles Ltd, Guildford and King's Lynn

Contents

Acknowledgements

This book is being published simultaneously in five European languages; while this will naturally symbolise both the breadth and diversity of the business applications described and the integrity of the underlying methodologies, it has nevertheless provided some challenging editorial issues. For their help in providing the material in the book, and in turning it into a tangible end result, I would like to thank:

- the client organisations throughout Europe which have provided the opportunities and case studies on which each chapter is built;
- Alain Mitrani and Murray Dalziel, who as overall managing editors defined the core content and structure and drove forward a timetable which met commercial deadlines;
- professional colleagues in McBer & Co, Boston, US – particularly Lyle Spencer – for their visionary leadership, guidance and support during the last five years;
- professional colleagues in Hay UK who have helped shape my thoughts for my own contribution;
- my fellow contributors, for their cooperation under tight deadlines;
- Vicky Hibbert, for her overall editorial assistance;
- Sarah Buckley and Agnes Carlet-Lemee, for their specific help in anglicising particular contributions;

- Pauline Goodwin and Jo O'Driscoll of Kogan Page, for their advice and guidance;
- Sarah Hall and my family for handling equably innumerable international calls, messages and faxes.

David Fitt
Editor, English Language Edition
August 1992

The Contributors

The contributors of the material in this book are experienced human resources consultants based in five of Hay Group's sixteen European country operations. While they are all members of the professional network within Hay which focuses on human resource planning and development – building on approaches originated by McBer and Co, Hay Group's centre of research and technical excellence in this area of management – the raw materials for their chapters come from their own wide-ranging experience as consultants and managers. The only criterion for successful human resources development work is its contribution to organisational performance; the materials here are based exclusively on projects commissioned by Hay clients whose specific identity, for reasons of confidentiality and consistency, we have chosen to keep anonymous. To these many clients we are particularly indebted.

Annick Bernard leads Hay France's management development programmes in Paris. She has a substantial background in human resources work as a specialist working in industry and service organisations and, more recently, in consulting, where her area of special interest is individual and collective performance.

Charles Bethell-Fox currently leads Hay's human resource planning and development work in Canada, but at the time of writing his chapter was principal consultant with Hay in London. With a particularly strong academic background in occupational psychology and assessment, Dr Bethell-Fox's contribution is based on a number of client assignments where quantifiable improvements in performance have been demonstrated.

Antonio Carretta is the practice leader for human resource planning and development in Hay Italy. Following wide-ranging professional and managerial experience in industrial and service companies, his consulting work concentrates on assessment, career pathing, succession planning and performance management.

Murray Dalziel is managing director of Hay Management Consultants in London. He was formerly president and general manager of the International and Training Aids Division of McBer and Co. Dr Dalziel has specialised in human resource development for technical professionals and in organisational improvement programmes.

David Fitt is director of human resource planning and development in Hay UK and is also accountable for ensuring the effective integration of the various methodologies used by Hay across the human resource consulting spectrum. His managerial background is in the airline and chemical industries and his contribution here is based on innovative client projects in the energy, aerospace and financial sectors.

Frank Hartle leads Hay's work in performance management in the UK. With a background in teaching and educational administration, he has led major projects implementing performance management processes in a range of large and smaller organisations in the private and public sectors.

Tjerk Hooghiemstra leads Hay Group's human resource planning and development practice in Europe. With managerial experience principally in the finance sector, he has led projects in the Netherlands and Europe on management development and organisation review and change.

Alain Mitrani is director of human resource planning and development with Hay Management Consultants in Paris. He has led numerous competency-based projects as well as multi-disciplinary projects with a broader organisational impact.

Manfred Strombach is the practice leader for human resource planning and development in Hay Frankfurt. After early managerial experience, he became general manager of an international Management Development Association before moving into his current role.

Introduction

Releasing Value Through People

Murray M Dalziel
Managing Director, Hay Group, UK

Organisations throughout Europe are using human resource practices to gain access to and develop the skills they need to be successful. These practices are critical if employers are to unlock the real talents that their workforces contain.

The type of practices that we focus on include:

- identifying the right skills and qualities for success in today's environment;
- selecting the best performers and people with the greatest potential;
- planning to meet individual and organisational needs;
- appraising performance and skills acquisition;
- paying for skills;
- building the best working environment and collective performance;
- managing motivation for improved performance.

The practices and approaches described are drawn from the experience of Hay/McBer consultants in Europe in client organisations covering a wide spectrum of sectors, cultures, services and geography. They reflect a growing recognition that, as we approach the end of the twentieth century, the world of work is changing. What has emerged is that the people doing the work are just as important as the work itself. This is why this book concerns itself with the interaction of work people and organisations.

A new focus for a new decade

For many countries the 1980s was the decade of fast growth, wealth creation, performance and even greed. Yet today a new focus is emerging. When commentators come to summarise the 1990s they will talk about the decade of value, quality and 'community'. If our organisations do not move fast enough to grasp this change then events will leave them behind.

The context for creating wealth is different now. Throughout this century we have built huge enterprises across the developed world. We are no longer searching for new markets or trade routes; we are no longer building new industrial or service enterprises; we are no longer rebuilding this part of Europe after war. Wealth creation over the last century has been fuelled by these activities. The task of the 1990s will be to tap into these enormous enterprises and realise their true value.

Before this decade we sought wealth creation by looking outside our enterprises. In the 1990s the winners will be those companies that unlock the value that is theirs already – their people, their practices and their systems.

The way to release value

This book focuses on working methods that help organisations to realise value. There are a number of ways in which this can be done. The rise of information technologies has changed the structure of work in many industries. Yet such changes are never successful unless managers really address the issues concerning people. These are issues that range from establishing appropriate skill levels in changing roles to understanding how new work structures can meet people's motivation needs.

Companies will depend on a rigorous re-examination of their organisational structures to release value. There is now a huge emphasis on 'delayering'. Bureaucratic procedures and high levels of reporting relationships are disappearing in less hierarchical 'flatter' organisations. Nevertheless, these changes will never achieve their purpose unless the organisations confront the issues concerning people. For example, in structures where those who perform tasks control decisions, they need the capability to deal with increasing and more flexible workloads.

Other companies will see total quality as their way of releasing value. Some sections of the total quality movement have moved dramatically away from merely concentrating on technical measurement to more all-embracing schemes for looking at the people and organisational issues. Technical measurement alone is not enough to produce total quality.

Practical methods

Aiming at being practical, this book is intended for both human resource professionals and for managers, as they are concerned, in the broadest sense, with the best possible use of individuals within their organisations.

Rather than imposing a common style on the various contributions to this book and systematically excluding material that in some way duplicates or is inconsistent with approaches in other chapters, we have preferred to preserve originality and diversity. This demonstrates that, far from being in conflict, varied approaches depict the same reality from different perspectives.

But this was only possible because powerful 'unifying' concepts support the diversity of implementation. The central theme – the notion of competency – serves as our leitmotiv and underpins all the contributions. These principles, and the overall organisation of the material in the book, were developed by Alain Mitrani.

Competencies – throughout human resources applications

Many organisations have gone down the route of carefully defining the attributes and skills they need for this new world. Some companies see these as their cultural hallmark. This is an important step towards identification of the pivotal skills or competencies that really describe what makes people successful in given roles or situations. Tjerk Hooghiemstra's chapter describes a working approach to defining these competencies for the future.

In many organisations the personnel department has been the last to change its structure. However, in the new European organisation a common language will integrate the management of human resources, as the chapters by Charles Bethell-Fox, Manfred Strombach and Antonio Carretta point out. Each looks at a different part of the human resource system. They write from different geographical backgrounds and with different types of organisation in mind, yet the core technique of looking at the fundamental qualities of people remains the same. Selection systems, appraisal systems, evaluation systems, succession planning and career planning systems can use fundamentally the same language.

Many organisations today expect to release value from people through well-constructed programmes in which managers and employers can be clear about objectives and the other criteria that will make performance happen in that organisation. But objective based performance management schemes will not be sufficient for the future. The future will involve continuous improvement where success is not so much about goal attainment, described by concrete targets, as about demonstrating qualities and behaviours associated with high performance. This requires new ways of thinking about managing the performance and careers of employees. Frank Hartle's chapter describes that type of approach. David Fitt discusses the dilemmas of paying for these attributes.

Many companies today have gone down the route of radically changing their culture. Some have been successful but the future organisation will not depend so much on top down visionary leadership so much as emphasising behaviour and changing individual responses to situations. The chapter by Annick Bernard describes this approach.

The new Europe will still consist of companies with distinctive cultures. But one thing will be clear: the winners will be those companies that embrace the concept of releasing value in their people. Our hope is that this book will give some insights to managers and human resource professionals on working methods to help their organisations do this.

1

Integrated Management of Human Resources

Tjerk Hooghiemstra
Hay Group, The Netherlands

In this chapter we look at the need for an integrated human resource management strategy and show how it can be achieved. The successful organisation of the future will be a new shape, requiring new attitudes from managers and employees. This chapter shows how competencies can be identified, measured and developed to become the building blocks of the winning organisation of the future. We give the history and definition of competencies and provide a review of how they can be used in all parts of human resources management.

FUTURE ORGANISATIONS: CLUSTERS

Organisations in the future will be flatter than those of today. Traditional hierarchical relations will be replaced by networks of 'empowered' work groups. Information will be at everyone's fingertips rather than being available only to those at the strategic apex of the organisation. Careers will increasingly become a sequence of different assignments rather than a sequence of different job titles representing a climb to the top.

In this context employees are beginning to work in cluster organisations where people are not tied to a management level by traditional hierarchical lines[1]. These clusters have a great amount of freedom in which to accomplish a mission given to them. The performance of these empowered clusters is measured on the accomplishment of the mission only. To make this kind of organisation successful four conditions are required:

- mission;
- competence;
- information;
- culture.

Mission
Providing leadership is a responsibility for people at the top of a flat organisation but flatter and more professional organisations are not necessarily highly participative nor need they be undirected. Clarity about the mission of the entire organisation and of the cells in a network or cluster organisation is a prerequisite for the success of these organisations.

Competence
The organisation of the future will be built around people. There will be much less emphasis on jobs as the building blocks of organisations. This means that increased attention will be focused on people's competence. If we are using people as the building blocks of the organisation, then what they bring to the job, in other words their competence, becomes crucial.

Information
If work groups that have a large amount of freedom to decide how best to accomplish their mission are not provided with access to information, they will fall back on classical hierarchical 'do what I tell you' styles of operating.

Culture
Cluster organisations will depend for their success on the willingness of people to be accountable for the larger tasks that are delegated to

their cluster. This accountability will require them to take calculated risks and accept responsibility for their actions without being able to devolve the ultimate responsibility to management level. This requires a management culture in which initiatives and calculated risks taken to accomplish the mission are appreciated. People should feel free to show this behaviour without having to fear the consequences for their career.

COMPETENCE: A CRITICAL FACTOR

To benefit fully from the opportunities the new types of organisation provide, a more integrated form of human resource management, based on a clear notion of required competence for success in roles (rather than jobs), is needed. This will require a much sharper image of the real strengths and weaknesses of people against the background of these insights. Deepening the insight on competencies and building an integrated human resource management on this foundation is also a key success factor for at least two out of the three conditions described above. Managers will have to be developed who can really take up the mission-providing leadership role described. What is the point of having information if one does not know what to do with it?

It is often startling to see the superficial basis on which decisions regarding people are taken in companies, especially for example, when compared with decisions regarding capital investment. The overall theme of this chapter will be that, when it comes to people, organisations must improve their decision making dramatically.

The following example shows how the failure to analyse people's competence can affect not only their jobs but also the organisation.

Case 1: Promotion beyond competence

At the age of 25, John was employed by a large software firm. He had just completed his study of information/computer science with excellent results and therefore could choose from various job offers. His employer was extremely happy with him and classed him as 'high-potential'. His first job proved to be a great success.

From the beginning he was one of the best system designers in the team. The following table (Figure 1.1) shows John's score on a selection questionnaire in combination with the job demands.

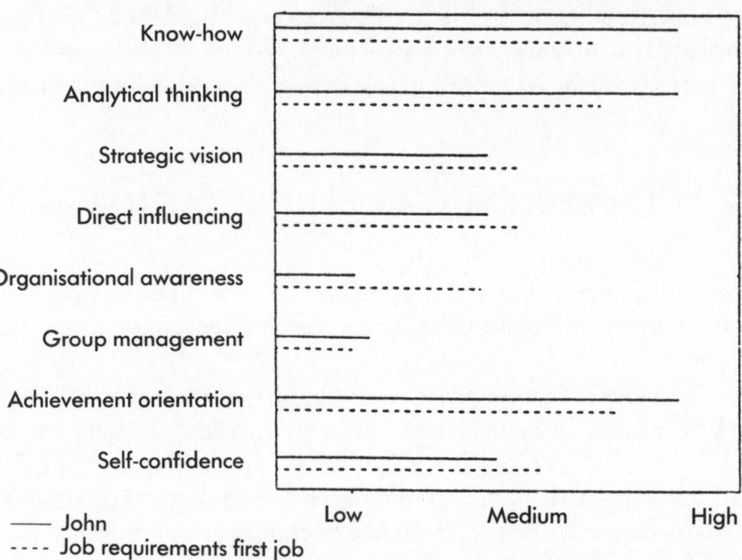

Figure 1.1 John versus the job requirements of his first job

This example shows that John fitted in well with the job demands. His know-how and ability to think in an analytical way and his strong competitive spirit made him most suitable. Although he lacked a few management competences, it was no surprise that he was an excellent performer in this job. His career proceeded successfully. He carried out larger projects and showed that he could handle them well. It seemed that he grew to the occasion and the more difficult the project, the better he performed. In the end, after a few stages, he had become the technical manager of the software firm. Expectations were high as John was still considered to be high-potential.

In the early days of his new job as a manager of managers all seemed well, but after a time his performance lacked a certain acuteness of judgement. An increasing number of important decisions were taken without consulting him. There were complaints that John should concentrate on the broad outlines of policy and not on details of projects.

The important question is how could this have happened? His start was excellent and he held several managerial posts with great success. Figure 1.2 shows John's profile in comparison with the job demands of his last job.

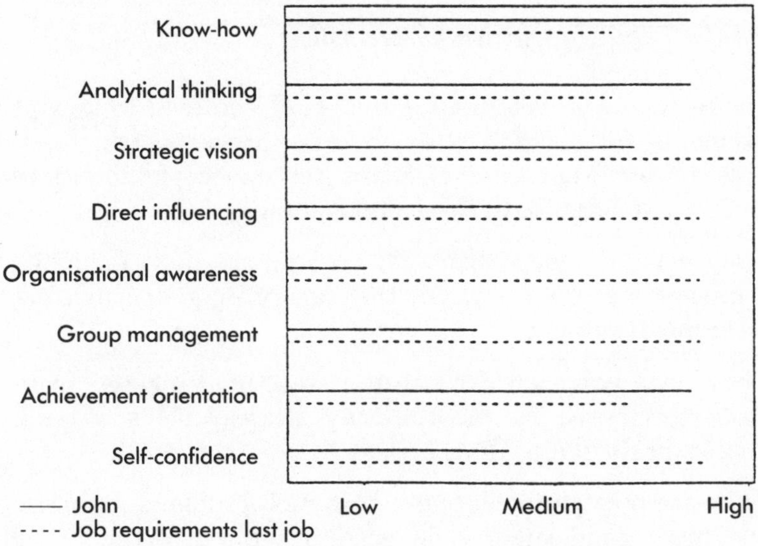

Know-how
Analytical thinking
Strategic vision
Direct influencing
Organisational awareness
Group management
Achievement orientation
Self-confidence
—— John
- - - - Job requirements last job
Low Medium High

Figure 1.2 John versus the job requirements of his last job

In comparison with his previous job, his new role required a much greater independent development of a vision and the ability to make people enthusiastic about it. This job did not really challenge his expertise and mental acuteness. He concentrated too much on the contents of the projects and too little on the business environment, both in a strategic and organisational sense. As a result of this his isolation increased and he could not exert any real influence. He preferred to do everything himself. The essence of the problem is really that John is motivated to excel himself instead of managing others so that they can excel.

He can still function, but the chance is great that he will not feel happy and that his contribution towards the company is not as great as it could be. This is a clear case of an inappropriate use of talent.

How many good system designers have walked into this trap? How many good sales people have become sales managers and subsequently discovered that the job is beyond their abilities? Everyone working in an organisation will recognise the problem. So why does it still exist?

Reasons for failure in selection for promotion

There are two main reasons for this. First, we tend to look at the requirements for success in a job in a rather unstructured and unfocused way. Many organisations set up people specifications; however, these often have three disadvantages:

- They make too many demands on a prospective candidate. The company does not know whether or not these demands are the most important ones.
- They have not been derived in a structured manner from the challenges posed by the company strategy. This is especially important for senior functions.
- They are not specific enough. Many job profiles summarise the qualities a candidate should possess, without explicitly stating what these qualities *are*. A frequently occurring demand is for 'social skills', but exactly what is meant by 'social skills'? Does it mean being a nice person; taking an interest in other people; good manners; or being able to integrate others in groups? Knowing this will make it easier to select the ideal candidate.

Secondly, during selection procedures a short-term orientation often dominates. Both with internal and external selection of people, there is a tendency to give insufficient weight to certain essential qualities that may be difficult to develop in some people.

If somebody does not demonstrate 'power' based qualities strongly, it will be very difficult to change this at a later phase in life but it is certainly necessary to do so if this person is destined to have managerial responsibilities. (In Case 1 this problem was very evident.)

The cause of this problem is that there is no real understanding of the job requirements, and the organisation does not know how they should be tested practically in a selection procedure.

The next case shows an organisation that, from a human resource management point of view, ran into a similar problem as in Case 1. It also shows a way to cope with these problems.

Case 2: Management trainees

A bank selected a few dozen young graduates each year. This was the profile of the people they were looking for:

- excellent study results;
- demonstrable interest in finance;
- good social skills;
- integrity;
- entrepreneurship;
- a wide range of talents;
- ambition;
- self-confidence;
- excellent presentation skills;
- analytical mind;
- guts;
- inspires confidence;
- broad interests;
- representativeness;
- persuasiveness.

After some time it was clear that no candidate could meet all these demands. Because of the breadth of the profile this was hardly surprising. In the end candidates were selected who fitted in best, although they only satisfied a few criteria. Questions were increasingly asked about the use of the selection criteria, because in practice the whole selection concentrated on one criterion: 'does the candidate fit in?'. Although this factor is most important (certainly instinctively), it is a much too superficial basis on which to select people for an entire career.

When this situation became clear, the organisation examined what really separated the best management trainees from the rest in practice: what they did differently and why it was that they were different from the others – ie which qualities were the basis of that behaviour. This study showed a number of interesting results:

- Outstanding academic results did not correlate with success as a management trainee. (Much research has been done on this topic, for example, in the 1960s at Harvard University similar results were found.)

- Many management trainees, as a result of the inadequate selection criteria, were selected because they 'looked good'. People were frequently engaged who had a high need for the development of friendly relations in their life and work and were less focused on performance. These often were not the most successful trainees.

- There were quite a few trainees with a high score on 'guts' and 'entrepreneurship' who did not feel happy in the fairly rigid structures of a bank. Apparently the makers of the profile perceived the bank culture as more entrepreneurial than could, in practice, be offered to these applicants.

- In general it became evident that an important selection criterion had been forgotten. All high scorers among the trainees had a strong achievement motivation. They were motivated by always surpassing their own criteria for performance. They showed behaviour in which the following elements occurred:

  — a very strong inclination to do things better all the time;
  — a preference to work on projects in which they were in charge;
  — a continuous need for challenging but realistic targets;
  — a great need for feedback on their own performance.

- The bank was lucky that a number of former trainees had already reached management positions. This made it possible to analyse which difficult-to-trace qualities made the difference between them and the rest. One of the central elements was the effective use of power. The best people believed in the use of power to influence people to do things and used it in an effective way to the benefit of the company. Power had not been selected as a required quality.

- An interesting quality possessed by virtually all high scorers, and lacking in their less successful colleagues, was accurate self-assessment. The best trainees could indicate their strong and weak points clearly: points they were improving and the weaknesses they needed to overcome. They also thought it important to be able to show vulnerability and were willing to receive feedback. They had asked more experienced managers (or other trainees) to help them learn. This behaviour, which had its origin in both their value patterns and in their curiosity about themselves, determined the pace and quality of their learning and thus their success.

On the basis of these insights a one-day assessment centre for the selection of new trainees was set up. There, specific data on candidates was collected using the qualities typical of the bank's own high fliers. It was also still possible to assess whether a trainee fitted in after his study. This, however, was only a marginal test after a candidate had been successful in the assessment centre.

This simple intervention considerably increased the quality of the management trainees engaged, shortened the learning curve and even reduced selection costs as a result of a better focus.

The underlying qualities of the successful trainees - which made the difference between success and failure - were their competencies.

COMPETENCIES: HISTORY AND DEFINITION

The concept of competencies is not new. In American industrial-organisational psychology especially, there has been a competency movement since the late 1960s and early 1970s[2].

At this time in American psychology, with a few exceptions, interest in personality traits was out of fashion. Authorities such as Ghiselli[3] argued that testable personality traits rarely showed correlations better than 0.33 (10% of the variance) with job performance. An increasing number of studies were published that showed that traditional academic aptitude and knowledge content tests, as well as school grades and credentials did not predict job performance or success in life[4] and were often biased against minorities, women and people from lower socio-economic strata[5].

These findings let to the identification of principles for doing research into competency variables that would predict job performance but were not biased (or were at least less biased) by race, sex or socio-economic factors. The most important of these principles were as follows. First, to compare people who were clearly successful in jobs or life outcomes of interest to the assessor with those who were less successful, and thus to identify those characteristics associated with success. Second, to identify the operant thoughts and behaviours causally related to these successful outcomes. That is, the measurement of competency should involve the individual reacting to open-ended situations rather than relying on respondent measures, such as self-report and multiple-choice tests that require the individual to choose one of several well-defined alternative responses to carefully structured situations. The best predictor of what a person can and will do is what he or she spontaneously thinks and does in an unstructured situation – or has done in similar past situations.

The challenge was to answer the question: if traditional aptitude measures do not predict job performance, what does? McClelland's response was, firstly, to request a criterion sample that included some clearly superior performers, and a contrasting sample of average and/or poor US foreign service information officers.

Secondly, McClelland and Dailey developed a technique, the behavioural event interview (BEI), that combined previous selection techniques in a new way (Flanagan's critical incident method, 1954, and McClelland's own thematic apperception test). Where Flanagan had been interested in identifying the task elements of jobs, McClelland was interested in the characteristics of the people who did a job well.

The BEI asks people to think of several important on-the-job situations in which things turned out well or poorly and then to describe these situations in exhaustive narrative detail, answering questions such as:

- What led up to the situation?
- Who was involved?
- What did you think about, feel, want to have happen in the situation?
- What did you do?
- What was the outcome?

Thirdly, McClelland and his colleagues thematically analysed BEI transcripts from successful and unsuccessful information officers to identify characteristics that differed between the two samples, generally behaviours shown by superior performers but not by average performers. Thematic differences are typically translated into objective scoring definitions that can be reliably coded by different observers.

BEI transcripts are then scored according to these definitions using CAVE (Content Analysis of Verbal Expression) to measure motivation[6]. CAVE coding enables investigators to count and test statistically for the significance of differences in the characteristics shown by superior and average performers in various jobs.

The results of early work showed that all kinds of non-academic competencies, such as being able to generate a number of promotional ideas, management skills, speed in learning political networks etc, did predict successful performance on the job and did not differ among candidates by race, sex or socio-economic status.

The essence of McClelland's radically new competency assessment approach to job analysis is that it studies the people who do the job well, and defines the job in terms of the characteristics and behaviours of these people rather than taking the traditional approach of analysing the elements of the job.

For example, most managerial jobs involve planning and organising. The interesting question is what leads a person to plan and organise well or efficiently. Competency research indicates that two underlying competencies are related to effective planning and organising: achievement motivation (an overriding concern with increasing efficiency) and analytical thinking (the ability to prioritise things to identify what should be done first, and what needs to be done at time 1, in order that a subsequent task may be done at time 2, thus enabling the project to be completed at time 3).

Further research using this competency assessment method led to the definition of competency and procedures for conducting competencey research studies.

DEFINITION OF A COMPETENCY

A competency is defined as 'an underlying characteristic of an individual which is causally related to effective or superior performance in a job'[7]. Differentiating competencies distinguish superior from average performers. Threshold or essential competencies are required for minimally adequate or average performance. The threshold and differentiating competencies for a given job provide a template for personnel selection, succession planning, performance appraisal and development.

Competencies can be motives, traits, self-concepts, attitudes or values, content knowledge, or cognitive or behavioural skills – any individual characteristic that can be measured or counted reliably and that can be shown to differentiate significantly between superior and average performers, or between effective and ineffective performers. The following definitions of the above characteristics may be given:

- **Motive:** the underlying need or thought pattern that drives, directs and selects an individual's behaviour; eg the need for achievement.
- **Trait:** a general disposition to behave or respond in a certain way; for instance with self-confidence, self-control, stress resistance or 'hardiness'.
- **Self-concept:** (attitudes or values) measured by respondent tests that ask people what they value, what they think they do or are interested in doing.
- **Content knowledge:** of facts or procedures, either technical (how to trouble-shoot a defective computer) or interpersonal (techniques for effective feedback), as measured by respondent tests. Most findings show that content knowledge by itself rarely distinguishes superior from average performers.
- **Cognitive and behavioural skills:** either covert (eg deductive or inductive reasoning) or observable (eg active listening skills).

Competencies can be related to performance in a simple causal flow model (see Figure 1.3) that indicates that motive, trait, self-concept and knowledge competencies aroused by a situation predict skilled behaviours, which in turn predict performance. Competencies include intention, action and outcome. For example, achievement motivation (a strong concern with doing better against an internal standard of excellence, and a concern for unique accomplishment) predicts entrepreneurial behaviours: goal-setting, taking personal responsibility for

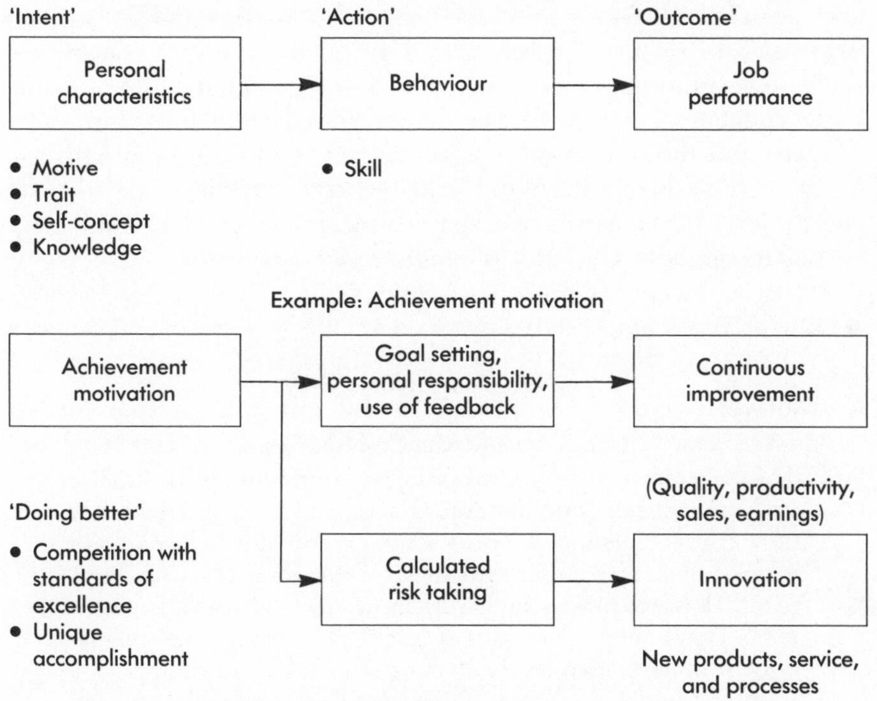

Figure 1.3 Competency casual flow model

outcomes, calculated risk taking.

In organisations, these behaviours lead to continuous improvement in quality, productivity, sales and other economic results and to innovation in the development of new products and services. Models provide managers with a simple way to do risk assessment in evaluating candidates for a job. The risk of hiring people without achievement motivation is that they will show less improvement in performance, less entrepreneurial behaviour and provide fewer ideas for new products or services.

Competencies differ in the extent to which they can be taught. Content knowledge and behavioural skills are easiest to teach. Altering attitudes and values is harder. While changing motives and traits is possible, the process is lengthy, difficult and expensive. From a cost-effectiveness standpoint, the rule is to hire for core motivation and trait characteristics and then develop knowledge and skills. Most organisations do the reverse: they hire on the basis of educational credentials (graduates from good schools and universities) and assume that candidates have, or can be indoctrinated with, the appropriate motives and traits. It is more cost-effective to hire people with the 'right stuff' and train them in the knowledge and skills needed to do specific jobs. In the words of one personnel manager, 'You can teach a turkey to climb a tree, but it is easier to hire a squirrel.'

Example of a competency

Interpersonal impact and influence

The most recent development in the research done by Hay/McBer on competencies is on developing scales on a set of frequently occurring competencies. These scales describe the behaviours of people ranging from those who possess the competency to a large extent down to those who hardly show any evidence of having it at all. The example given here is described in terms of behaviours on a scale with five levels. It is used to select successors to a country general manager position for a European wide information services group.

Definition

The desire to have an impact on others and the ability to affect others through strategies to persuade and influence. This includes calculating in advance the likely impact of one's words or actions and then selecting the words or actions most likely to have the desired effect; timing one's actions carefully to maximise their effectiveness and presenting a logical, compelling case or argument.

Rating

The person characteristically influences and persuades others in the following ways:

0. *Not applicable.* The person shows few or no attempts to influence and persuade.
1. *Intention.* The person attempts to have a specific effect or impact. For instance, he or she expresses concern with

reputation, status, appearance, etc; the person calculates how statements and actions will affect an audience.

2. *Direct persuasion*. The person takes a single action to persuade others in a discussion or presentation. For instance, he or she appeals to reason, data, others' self-interest, or a large purpose; the person uses concrete examples, visual aids or demonstrations. He or she adapts a presentation to the interest and level of the audience.
3. *Adaptive persuasion*. The person makes a two-step effort to influence – knowing when a particular strategy is not working well and shifting to an alternate one. (This usually includes careful preparation of data and control of the environment for a presentation.) He or she makes two or more different types of persuasive appeal in a presentation or discussion; or models desired behaviour; or takes one dramatic, unusual action to make an impact.
4. *Indirect influence*. The person marshals necessary resources over time in a planned effort. He or she uses experts or other third parties to influence; or takes three different actions; or makes complex, multi-stage arguments.
5. *Complete influence strategies*. The person uses complex strategies tailored to individual situations, often creating chains of indirect influence. For example, he or she influences or persuades someone so that this individual will influence others. The person structures jobs and situations in a way that encourages the desired behaviour.

COMPETENCY PROFILING

Competencies need to reflect the behaviour that is needed for the future success of the organisation. Figure 1.4 shows a process that consultants use a lot to help companies make the translation between strategic challenges and required behaviour and people's competencies.

Expert panel

In the expert panel the real translation between the challenges for the

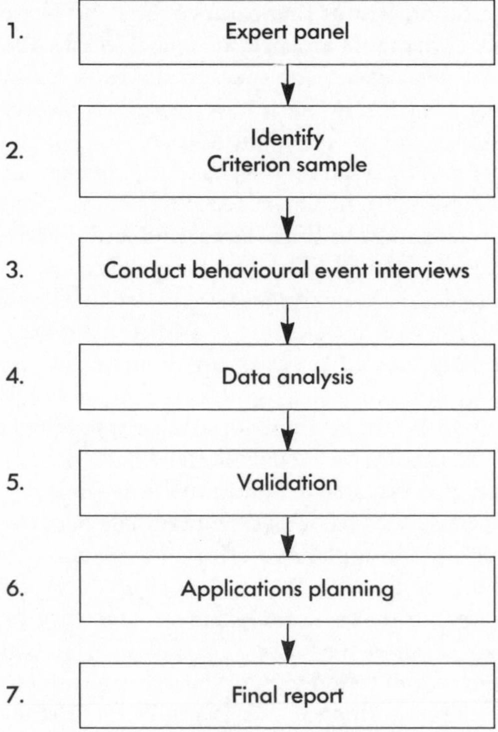

Figure 1.4 Competency model process

organisation and required behaviour is made. In the panel a group of knowledgeable human resource specialist managers and superior incumbents on various jobs with a clear picture of the future participate. The outline of the process is roughly as follows:

1. Vision building/agreeing on the challenges for the future based on a group discussion on strengths, weaknesses, opportunities, threats and key success factors for the organisation.
2. Reaching consensus about the mission for the job(s), roles, or a group of people that will be looked at in the expert panel, against a background of the strategic challenges.
3. Identification of required behaviours and competencies of these people against the background of the results of step 2. In this

step various techniques can be used; for instance job competency requirement inventories (questionnaires that search for a set of frequently occurring behaviours and competencies), a checklist of these behaviours and competencies or an expert system that allows the group to respond to questions posed by it. These questions are keyed in to an extensive database of competencies identified by previous studies. The expert system manages the analysis process and provides a detailed description of competencies required for adequate and superior performance in the job at hand.

4. Identification of a number of incumbents in the organisation who already show the competencies and behaviours that have emerged as a result of the deliberations of the expert panel. These incumbents are identified in step 2.

Behavioural event interviews

The use of competency profiles is aimed at describing behaviour (required as well as observed in people in the organisation) in specific terms that will provide a solid foundation for human resources management. This means collecting examples of real life behaviour. This is done by conducting a series of behavioural event interviews with a sample of people who show the kind of performance that has been defined by the expert panel as important for the future success of the organisation.

The sample of incumbents who are consistently rated superior on a number of different performance criteria provide a standard for comparison analysis with a sample of average performers. Ideally, each job study sample should include at least 20 subjects: 12 superior and 8 average performers. A total number of 20, permits simple statistical tests of hypotheses about competencies. Smaller samples, such as six superior and three average performers, cannot be statistically validated but can provide valuable qualitative data on the expression of competencies in a given organisation. For example, the data can show how influence is used effectively in the company. Small samples should include more superior than average performers (ie a ratio of two superior performers to one average performer) because the rule of competency research is, 'You always learn most from your superstars'.

Behavioural event interviews provide a wealth of data for the identification of competencies and very specific descriptions of critical job behaviours in specific situations. Interviewees' career paths can be mapped and some estimate made of when, where and how they acquired key competencies. An important by-product of these interviews is the generation of numerous situation and problem narratives that can be used to develop highly relevant training materials (eg case studies, role playing and simulations). Advantages of the BEI method include:

- empirical identification of competencies beyond or different from those generated by the expert panels;
- precision about what competencies are and how they are expressed in specific jobs and organisations (eg not only use of influence, but also examples of how influence is used to deal with a specific situation in a specific organisation's political climate);
- freedom from racial, gender and cultural bias – indeed, the BEI assessment approach has been adapted by many organisations because it predicts successfully without being biased against minority candidates.

Data analysis

All data from the previous steps is analysed by content to build a clear understanding and description of the competencies that will be used as the foundation for the human resources' applications. The descriptions of actual situations and behaviours given by the people who have been interviewed serve as examples to bring the definitions of the competencies to life.

Validation

The model can be validated by doing a second series of behavioural event interviews on a new group of people and checking whether the competencies identified correlate with the superior performance as identified by the expert panel. Competency models are a good core around which to build a logically interlinked set of human resource policies and techniques.

COMPETENCY MODELS AND THE INTEGRATED APPROACH

The next chapter of this book looks in more depth at constructing an integrated human resource management strategy. This chapter confines itself to a brief overview. Figure 1.5 shows the integrated human resource management elements around the competency model.

Recruitment and selection

Competency-based recruiting systems usually focus on screening methods that can be used to select a small number of strong candidates from a large group of applicants quickly and efficiently. Assessing

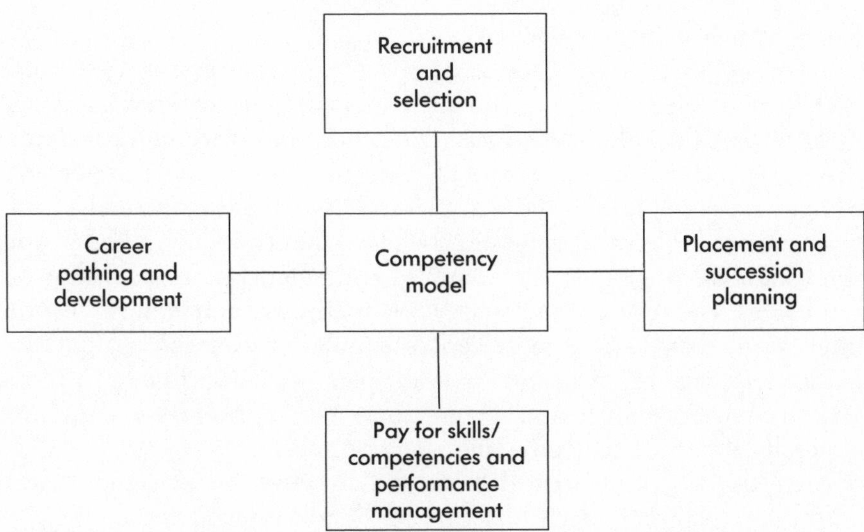

Figure 1.5 Integrated HRM around a clear understanding of core competencies

recruits involves special challenges, such as screening many applicants in a short period of time and eliminating those applicants who have just graduated from college and thus have little work experience on which to base judgements. Competency-based recruiting systems, therefore, stress identification of a few (three to five) core competencies that meet the following criteria:

- Competencies that applicants have already developed and demonstrated in their working lives (eg initiative).
- Competencies that are likely to predict a candidate's long-term prospects for success and that are hard to develop through employer's training or job experience (eg such master competencies as achievement motivation).
- Competencies that can be reliably assessed using a short, targeted behavioural event interview, for example, if collaborative team leadership is a desired competency, interviewees might be asked to give an example of their being able to get a group to do a particular activity. Their responses would then be coded for consensus-building versus adversarial behaviours.

Placement and succession planning

Competency-based placement and succession planning systems are best focused on identifying the top candidates for an organisation's most important value-added jobs. Selection and placement systems should, therefore, stress careful identification of the most important competencies required by critical jobs and then use as many sources of information about candidates as possible to determine whether or not the candidate possesses the required competencies. Assessment of candidates can involve a variety of methods: behavioural event interviews, tests, assessment centre simulations, review of performance appraisal reports, and superior, peer and subordinate ratings. Past job performance and behavioural event interview data are generally the most cost-effective selection tools.

Analysis of assessment data to make selection, placement and succession planning decisions can be done either manually or by computer systems that compare all candidates' ratings on competencies found to be essential or desirable for superior job performance.

Employees are recommended in rank order based on their total weighted scores on the competency criteria. Application planning for competency-based placement or succession includes: identification of the necessasry competencies, given the pool of candidates and the resources of the selection system; identification of the most cost-effective candidate assessment methods; training of assessors in behavioural event interviews and design of the selection system database, including the candidate pool, administration and tracking systems; and follow-up evaluation of those selected to ensure the effectiveness of the system.

Career development

The competency requirements for career pathing and development jobs or groups of jobs define a template for development. Employees who are appraised as lacking in a particular competency can be directed to a specific development activity designed to teach them the missing competency in order to improve their performance in their existing jobs, or to prepare them to advance to other assignments in the future. Competency development options include assessment centre experiences (employees' self-knowledge about competencies needing development, account for a significant part of the training's effect), formal training courses, developmental job assignments/career pathing, mentor relationships and the like.

For example, if John in Case 1 (p 19) is assessed as lacking in organisational influence skills, he might be offered a developmental assignment working as an aide to a senior manager known for his or her political astuteness.

A competency acquisition process (CAP) has been developed for increasing levels of competencies[8]. It includes the following components:

- **Recognition:** a simulation or case study that leads participants to recognise one or more competencies that predict superior performance in their jobs that they may have to learn;
- **Understanding:** specific instruction, including behaviour modelling, as to what the competency is and what it looks like in application;

- **Assessment:** feedback to participants about how much of the competency they have (determined by comparing superior performers' scores to the participants' scores); this is designed to motivate participants to learn the competency by making them aware of any gap between actual and ideal performance;
- **Practice/feedback:** exercise in which participants practice the competency and get feedback on how they perform against the superior performance level;
- **Job application:** participants set goals and develop specific action to use the competency in real life.

Pay for skills/competencies and performance management

Competency-based performance management systems add to traditional job performance standards and results. They measure those job behaviours required to accomplish specific job tasks and meet job responsibilities against competencies demonstrated by both average and superior performers in key jobs. Effective performance appraisal depends on the proper use of each type of data, given the objectives of the system and the degree of control employees have over their performance on the variables assessed. Performance results data are usually used for decisions about rewards (for instance, merit bonuses based on sales or production quotas). If, however, employees have little individual control over the final results (say, in a team production setting), rewards based solely on these results can demotivate superior performers. In these cases, some portion of the reward should be based on job behaviours.

Job behaviour data are usually used for decisions on skill development. For instance, if manager X's appraisal shows a lack of group leadership skills, he or she might be advised to attend a leadership course to develop this skill. Skill-based compensation systems also explicitly tie rewards to skills developed. This is particularly appropriate when employees have little control over performance results.

In the next case we look at an example of a company that put an integrated HRM approach together as has been advocated earlier in this chapter.

Case 3: Integrated human resources management at Euroservice

In the early 1980s Euroservice started a programme aimed at attaching much more importance to the performance of the individual worker. Under the title 'Performance '80' an extensive programme was started to extend the already existing management by objectives approach for business unit managers to the total population of workers. Targets derived from business plans and responsibilities in the jobs were formulated for all workers. A variable remuneration system was tied to achieving these individual targets. These were the results:

- the performance of the workers hardly improved;
- an unhealthy competition between workers obstructed team work;
- it was difficult to motivate people to make innovative contributions, because these were regarded as inherently risky.

Euroservice was surprised that the performance had not improved. Its management had foreseen potential difficulties with individual competition and risk avoiding behaviour and had hoped to circumvent this through senior managers taking corrective action. At this stage, there did not seem to be many possibilities to stimulate individual performance.

During the analysis of the disappointing results it emerged that the predominant cause of the problem was that managers had no idea *how* to direct performance. If a worker was in danger of not reaching his or her target, the manager could point this out. In the most favourable case the manager could offer the worker ideas on how to reach the agreed target. However, the manager could also do that before the introduction of Performance '80. In that sense little had changed. Managers were also aware of their task to stimulate team formation and innovative behaviour, but they did not know how to do this.

Euroservice was confronted with the essence of leadership: managers determine the difference. To enable managers to cope in practice, three things were done:

1. as well as individual performance targets, team targets were identified;
2. competency profiles were drawn up for 20 job clusters that included the entire organisation;
3. in training, the managers were made aware of the relationship between their own actions and the effects of these actions on the performance of teams and individuals.

Individual and team targets

The company wished to keep output as the primary focus in the work. Although Performance '80 was not a success, a clear output orientation had been developed that the company wished to retain. Subsequently, however, the variable income of the workers was no longer made dependent on achieving individual targets. When establishing the variable incomes, a mixture of company targets, team targets and individual targets was used. This mixture varied for each category of jobs and was formulated again each year during the budgeting rounds.

Competency profiles for 20 job clusters

One of the greatest objections to the system was that managers could only assess individual targets according to output criteria. They only assessed what they *expected* of people and not how these people could *achieve* these results. The latter is necessary to assist workers and as a result to direct the performance.

To solve this problem jobs were clustered. In the whole organisation 20 clusters were identified. For example: senior general management, middle general management, managers of professional groups, senior staff members, junior staff members, salespeople and so on. For these 20 groups competency profiles were compiled by means of the techniques described above. It was established which type of behaviour of job practitioners in these clusters led to success and which types of competency of high fliers were the cause of this success. With this information the managers could improve their staff performance considerably. Instead of telling salesperson X about a backlog in the realisation of a sales budget, the sales manager could, for example, together with the employee, see whether X had shown the influencing behaviour which, when drawing up the competency profile, had led the best sales people to their successes. Furthermore, the various competency profiles were also used in assessment centres for selection, defining the development paths of people and for identifying concrete training and education needs. In this way, an integrated human resources management system could be developed around one core understanding of the competencies identified as essential for the future success of the company.

Training of managers

One of the most important factors determining the behaviour of people is the climate in the work environment. If one's own freedom and responsibility are low, if the standards for performance are low, if workers are punished more than rewarded, if there is little pride and involvement, even those with the correct profile may still run dry. The challenge for the manager must be to prevent such a work climate developing and achieve a stimulating environment in which the best comes out in people. To meet this challenge the executive staff of Euroservice were trained according to *Managing Motivation for Performance Improvement*, a method described in Chapter 7. In this programme all managers were subjected to a three-fold assessment:

1. their own individual competency profile versus that of their job cluster;
2. their style of leadership;
3. the work climate in their work unit.

Next, they were confronted with the relationship that existed between these three aspects. The training is aimed at helping managers to shape their behaviour in such a way that it will result in the best possible work climate for the work unit.

COMPETENCIES FOR THE FUTURE

What can be said regarding the competencies needed to meet new challlenges and the new kind of organisations we will be working in the near future? From authors such as Spencer[9] and Howard we can derive the following insights into the qualities we will be looking for in people in these new organisations.

Executives

- **Strategic thinking** to understand rapidly changing environmental trends, market opportunities, competitive threats and the strengths and weaknesses of their own organisation, in order to identify the optimum strategic response.
- **Change leadership** to communicate a compelling vision of the firm's strategy that transforms employees into stakeholders, arousing their genuine motivation and commitment; to act as sponsors of innovation and entrepreneurship and to allocate the firm's resources in the best possible way to implement frequent changes.
- **Relationship management** to establish relationships with and influence complex networks of others in many countries whose co-operation is needed for the organisation to succeed but over whom one has no formal authority: product champions, customers, stockholders, labour representatives, government regulators at all levels (local, state and federal), legislators, interest groups.

Managers

- **Flexibility** to change managerial structures and processes when necessary to implement the organisation's change strategies.
- **Change implementation** to communicate the organisation's need for change to co-workers; and 'change management' skills, such as communication, training and group process facilitation, needed to implement change in their work groups.
- **Interpersonal understanding** to understand and value the inputs of many different types of people.
- **Empowering** by sharing information, soliciting co-workers' ideas, fostering employee development, delegating meaningful responsibility, providing coaching feedback, expressing positive expectations of subordinates (irrespective of differences) and rewarding performance improvement – all of these make employees feel more capable and motivated to assume greater responsibility.

- **Team facilitation** to get diverse groups of people to work together effectively to achieve a common goal, eg establishing goal and role clarity, giving everyone the chance to participate, resolving conflicts.
- **Portability** rapidly to adapt and function effectively in foreign environments – a manager must be 'portable' to positions anywhere in the world.

Employees

- **Flexibility** to see change as an exciting opportunity rather than a threat, eg the adoption of new technology should be seen as 'getting to play with new gadgets, the latest and best!'
- **Information seeking, motivation and ability to learn** is genuine enthusiasm for opportunities to learn new technical and interpersonal skills, eg the secretary who, when asked to learn to use a spreadsheet program and take over department accounting, welcomes this request as job enrichment rather than seeing it as an additional burden. This competency transcends computer literacy and other specific technical skills that future searchers are believed likely to need. It is the impetus for life-long learning of any new knowledge and skill required by the changing requirements of future jobs.
- **Achievement motivation** is the impetus for innovation: the continuous improvement in quality and productivity needed to meet (or better, lead) ever-increasing competition.
- **Work motivation under time pressure** is a combination of flexibility, achievement motivation, stress resistance and organisation commitment that enables individuals to work under increasing demands for (new) products and services in ever-shorter periods of time.
- **Collaborativeness** to work co-operatively in multi-disciplinary groups with diverse co-workers: positive expectations of others, interpersonal understanding, organisational commitment.
- **Customer service orientation** is a genuine desire to be of help to

others; interpersonal understanding sufficient to be aware of customers' needs and emotional state and sufficient initiative to overcome obstacles in one's own organisation to solve customer problems.

SUMMARY

This chapter is intended to suggest a framework for the successful management of human resources in the kind of organisations we will be working in in the coming years. In doing so, theories and concepts that have been around for quite some time have been utilised. There is logic behind this. The importance of human resource management in the next decade will force us to come up with proven solutions rather than experimenting with new vogue ideas that have only been superficially tested.

Another argument for using these concepts is that they are universal. There is no mystery about them, they are the most straightforward tools for looking at the jobs and roles people play in organisations. When put in the centre of our human resource management and used daily in our discussions about people, the clear descriptions of the behaviours become part of our business culture. Let us get back to the key success factors for the new cluster organisations:

1. mission;
2. competence;
3. information;
4. culture.

The message is that a competency-based human resource management could be of help in meeting three of these four requirements, namely to make sure that the organisation has managers who can take up the proper leadership in these organisations, that the employees know what to do with all the information they receive and that the competence needed for the success of the company is ensured in a structured and focused way. The notion that competencies become a vehicle for communication about values in the organisation leads us to the conclusion that this approach to human resource management might also help to realise a corporate culture in which initiative and calculated risk taking are appreciated.

Competency profiling and a set of interlinked applications for selection, succession planning, development, reward and performance management can be of great help in getting the most out of our new organisations and ourselves.

REFERENCES

1. Quinn Mills, D (1991) *Rebirth of the Corporation* John Wiley and Sons.
2. Spencer Jr, LM 'Job Competency Assessment', in Glass and Harold *Handbook of Business Strategy*, Warren, Gorham & Lamont, second edition.
3. Ghiselli, EE (1966) *The Validity of Occupational Aptitude Tests*, John Wiley and Sons.
4. McClelland, DC (1973) 'Testing for competence rather than for "intelligence"' *American Psychologist* vol 28, No 1, pp 1–4 American Psychological Association.
5. Fallows, J (1985) 'The case against credentialism' *The Atlantic Monthly* pp 49–67.
6. Zullow, HM, Oettingen, G, Peterson, C, and Seligman, ME (1988) 'Pessimistic explanatory style in the historical record' *American Psychologist* **43(9)** pp 673–82.
7. Boyatzis, RE (1982) *The Competent Manager*, John Wiley and Sons.
8. Spencer Jr, LM (1983) *Soft Skill Competences*, Edinburgh: Scottish Research Council on Education.
9. Spencer Jr, LM, McClelland, DC and Spencer SM (1990) *Competency Assessment Methods: History and State of the Art* Hay/McBer Research Press.

2

Career and Succession Planning

Antonio Carretta
Hay Management Consultants, Italy

This chapter examines human resource planning for the long term – both for careers within the organisation and for the most important top-level jobs.

First it will look at the changing expectations of employees and at how human resource planning systems match the organisation's goals with the needs of its people. The best way of matching people and jobs is through competency modelling; after this is explained, a step-by-step approach will show how to devise and operate career path and succession planning systems.

THE CHANGING EMPLOYEE

Companies are under more and more pressure to find ways to implement their strategies in a rapidly changing environment, where planning lifecycles tend to shrink to reduce the 'time-to-market' intervals. When the rate and quality of change exceed a certain threshold, the requirement of talented people to run the business cannot be described merely as manpower planning problems. The managerial and professional talent required often reflects the demands of a dramatically different work style from that which was previously typical in the company's culture.

Technological impact

Recent surveys conducted in Europe show the following main trends:

- people try more and more to match their work-related choices with a broader lifestyle, resulting in a more selective attitude to their occupation;
- people look for pleasure in their jobs, as against the traditional attitude of showing duty – they refuse either routine or unpleasant tasks;
- there is a growing interest in jobs that provide recognition and success, responding to the achievement needs of an increasing number of 'knowledge workers';
- professional links become tighter than organisational ones, resulting in a work style that demonstrates 'loyalty-to-profession' rather than to the 'life-long company' ideal.

This makes it difficult to ensure that an organisation has the right people in the right job at the right time – which was the main aim of manpower planning technology during the 1970s and early 1980s.

Impact of changing career paths

The traditional career models, now rapidly vanishing under pressure of change, were associated with vertical movement: in traditional, hierarchical organisations career paths were viewed as climbing up the corporate ladder, reaching the top of the pyramid. New corporate realities, including down-sizing, outplacement, flattening and the growth of entrepreneurship and total quality awareness, converge with new contemporary values, which are evolving to reflect a greater concern with flexibility, challenge and individual lifestyle than with steady linear advancement in the same organisation.

Multichannel career paths are beginning to emerge, in which there may be lateral or even downward movement from one work field to another if this change gives the individual the chance to acquire knowledge, personal development and freedom of choice. Also appearing is the 'self-designing organisation'[1], defined as one facing rapidly changing environments by means of improvisation, continued adaptation, generalist managers (rather than specialists) and networks. These organisations focus on skills, metaskills and behaviours, ie competencies, that individuals are expected to acquire and master, to deal with change. It is not enough merely to attend from 9 to 5 to get the job done.

HUMAN RESOURCE PLANNING SYSTEMS

The human resource planning system (HRPS) is a way in which companies try to align organisation and people to achieve business goals. The methods and tools involved are illustrated in Figure 2.1. The

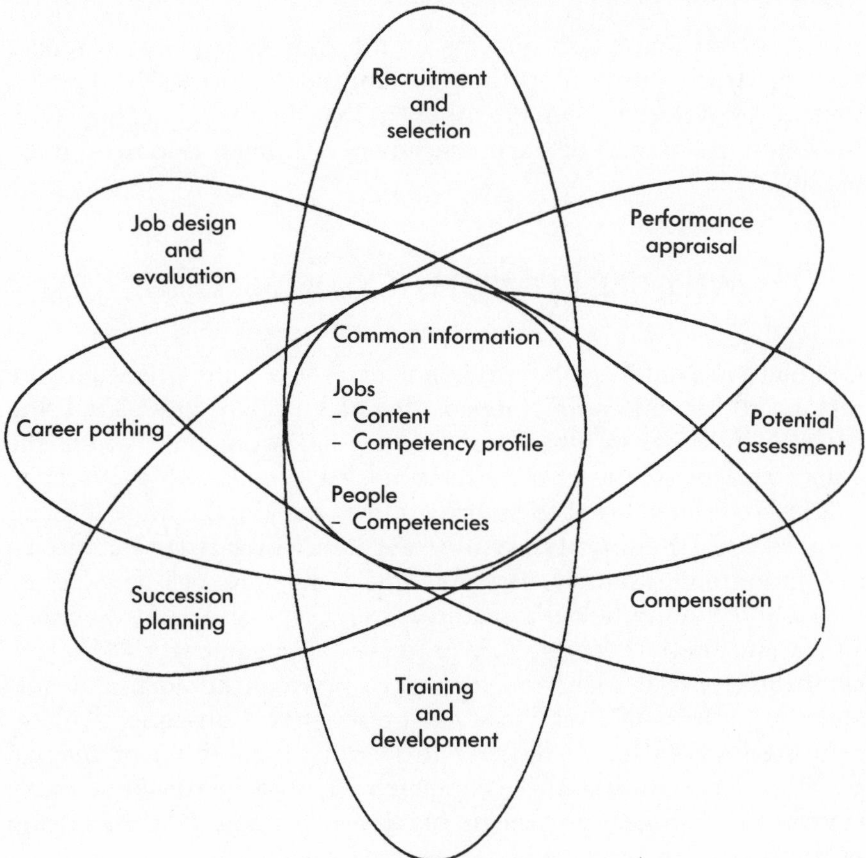

Figure 2.1 Human resource planning system

system involves many sub-systems relating to 'hard' organisational variables (those concerning jobs and careers) as well as 'soft' ones (those concerning people).

Some of these sub-systems are information suppliers that give the HRPS consistent data to work on; others deal with human resources. They are as follows:

- performance appraisal and monitoring system for potential;
- recruitment and selection system;
- training and development programmes;
- competitive compensation systems.

The two remaining sub-systems of the human resource planning system, namely the career pathing system and the succession planning system, are different from the others in that they are concerned with the long-term aspects of the management of human resources in the organisation.

WHY USE COMPETENCY MODELLING?

Optimal job–person matching is not easy at a time when jobs are tending to become more complex. Defined jobs are gradually being replaced by those in which no one but the incumbent can tell the extent and the nature of the efforts needed to make things work.

Research shows[2] that the more complex the job, the more difficult it is to identify the critical tasks and competencies related to success. To use an extreme example, assembly line tasks may well be circumscribed and the job holder's required knowledge and skills described simply and briefly. In contrast, in professional and managerial jobs, the competencies that make the difference between minimal and outstanding performance tend to be less prescriptive. Consequently these competencies are more difficult to identify than those of manual workers. Nevertheless, these competencies must be considered very closely throughout the design of career pathing and succession planning of professional and managerial jobs.

A better understanding of the tasks and competency requirements of the various jobs that form a career path helps to clarify human resource planning and to identify those transitions of roles that involve a professional jump that is not only quantitative but also qualitative.

Two jobs may have functional similarities yet there may be little overlap in the competency profile needed for effective performance. The most commonly cited example of this phenomenon is that of the transition from salesperson to sales manager: people in these two jobs share tasks, yet the role of sales manager demands competencies that are quite different from those required by the salesperson's job.

Another case in which competency-based career paths become useful is when job structure is subject to frequent changes in tasks and goals. Competency-based career paths help to build a basis for human resource planning that will still be effective, even when processes and functions change in their more superficial aspects.

COMPETENCY-BASED CAREER PATHS

Career pathing involves making a series of job–person matches, based on the demands of the job system in the organisation, that enable the person to grow into greater levels of responsibility, thus providing the organisation with the talent that it requires to meet goals. This should involve the careful assignment of an individual to positions that provide her or him with opportunities for deploying the competencies needed for a more challenging position.

Best approaches to career pathing combine an analysis of positions in terms of both the tasks and the organisational behaviours needed for superior performance. The combined approach is essential for each of the jobs in the chain, because there may be marked differences between the characteristics demanded in one job and those needed in another in the same career path.

Steps to implement the system

The major steps in developing a competency-based career pathing system are:

1. Put together a resource panel of experts on the target and feeder jobs who will set direction and specify the expected job performance criteria.
2. Define tasks and characteristics, through the resource panel, and survey job incumbents to obtain their perceptions of which job tasks and personal characteristics contribute to success in the target and feeder jobs.
3. Identify top performers in the target and feeder jobs, using performance criteria specified by the panel.
4. Conduct in-depth interviews with both superior and average incumbents in the target and feeder jobs to find out what they do and how they do it (see the behavioural event interview technique addressed in Chapter 1).
5. Based on the outcome of stage 4, develop a competency model of people in the target and feeder jobs by identifying those competencies that make the biggest contribution to outstanding performance as opposed to the competencies that all job holders need.
6. Analyse career paths by combining the survey (stage 2) and the interview (stage 3) results for target and feeder jobs.
7. Implement the career pathing system through a number of options as we have already seen in Chapter 1:
   - computer-based tasks and competency inventories;
   - performance and potential assessment linked to new job opportunities;
   - systematic counselling;
   - career development and related training programmes.

Figure 2.2 shows a career path diagram displaying main job families in a huge EDP Centre. Each job family is connected to the others in a step by step mode and is labelled with main 'differentiators' against the next possible job in the organisation chain. Each job further along in the career path requires the holder to master the preceding competencies. For example, the job of project team leader demands concern for order, analytical thinking, group management, self-confidence and self-control, plus the specific technical expertise relating to the software and hardware environments.

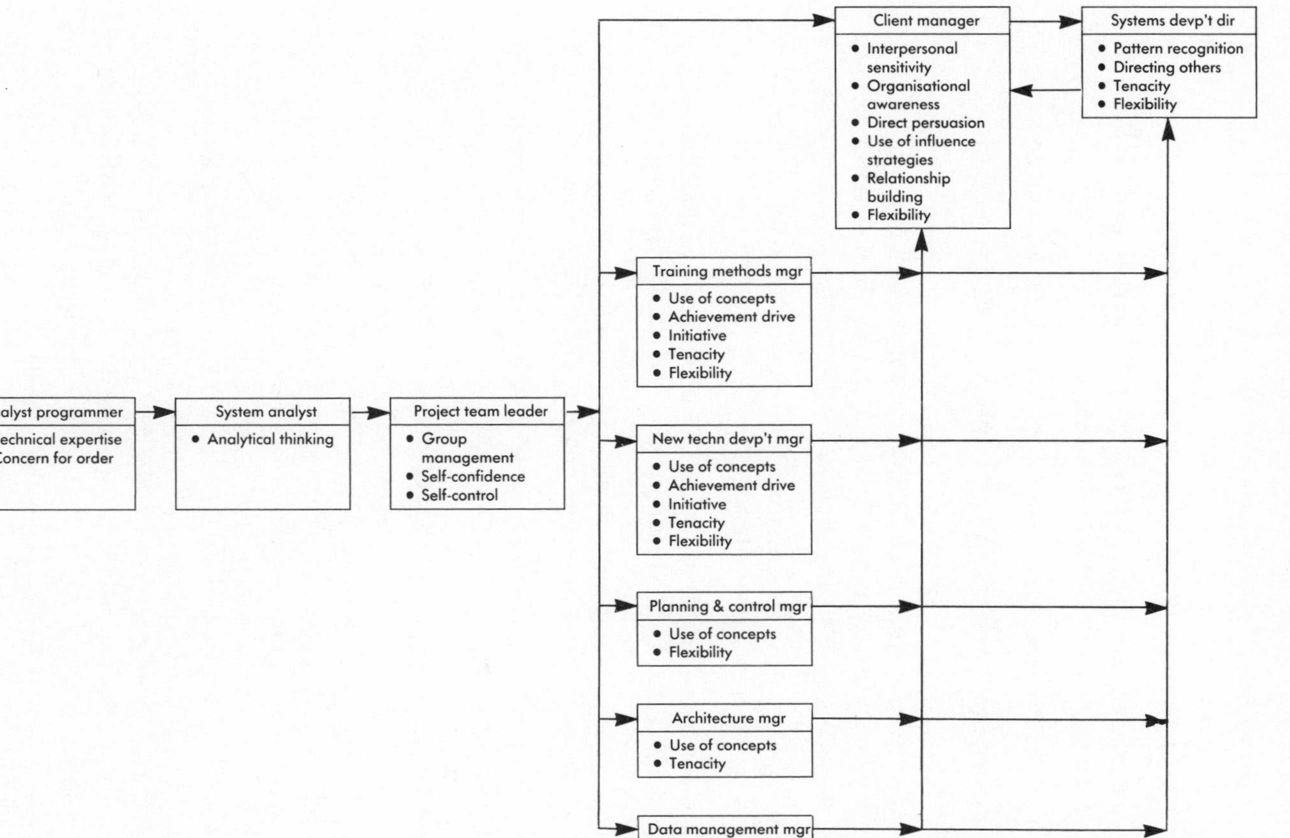

Figure 2.2 Career path in EDP Centre

Tools of the system

The tools of a competency-based career pathing system include:

- a description of the tasks required by target and feeder jobs eventually broken down by job families;
- a competency model for the target and feeder job system;
- a dictionary of behavioural descriptions of each competency in the model;
- performance indicators that provide the material for a competency-based evaluation programme and a computerised skills bank (see also 'just noticeable differences' in Chapter 3);
- a competency profile grid for either internal or external recruiting and selection of candidates;
- a career map of the organisation, identifying which jobs are the key feeders to higher-level positions;
- a competencies' gap analysis showing main differences required to flow through the job system to reach high-level jobs;
- recommendations for training in or selecting for each competency in the path.

Figure 2.3 shows a career path for the design and operation of a high-tech satellite transmission system. In this example the company aimed at developing career mobility among a population of highly specialised researchers and engineers who were blocked in their career paths because of early in-depth specialisation into narrow areas of expertise. In this case the competency model explored not only personal characteristics but also the nature and depth of technical know-how required to perform highly sophisticated jobs.

Combining both behavioural and technical requirements produced a framework linking different departments that showed the kind of professional empowerment that was needed to switch from one specialised mainstream to the other (Figure 2.4).

Each job family was then analysed to provide its own specific developmental sheets: the training and developmental activities that

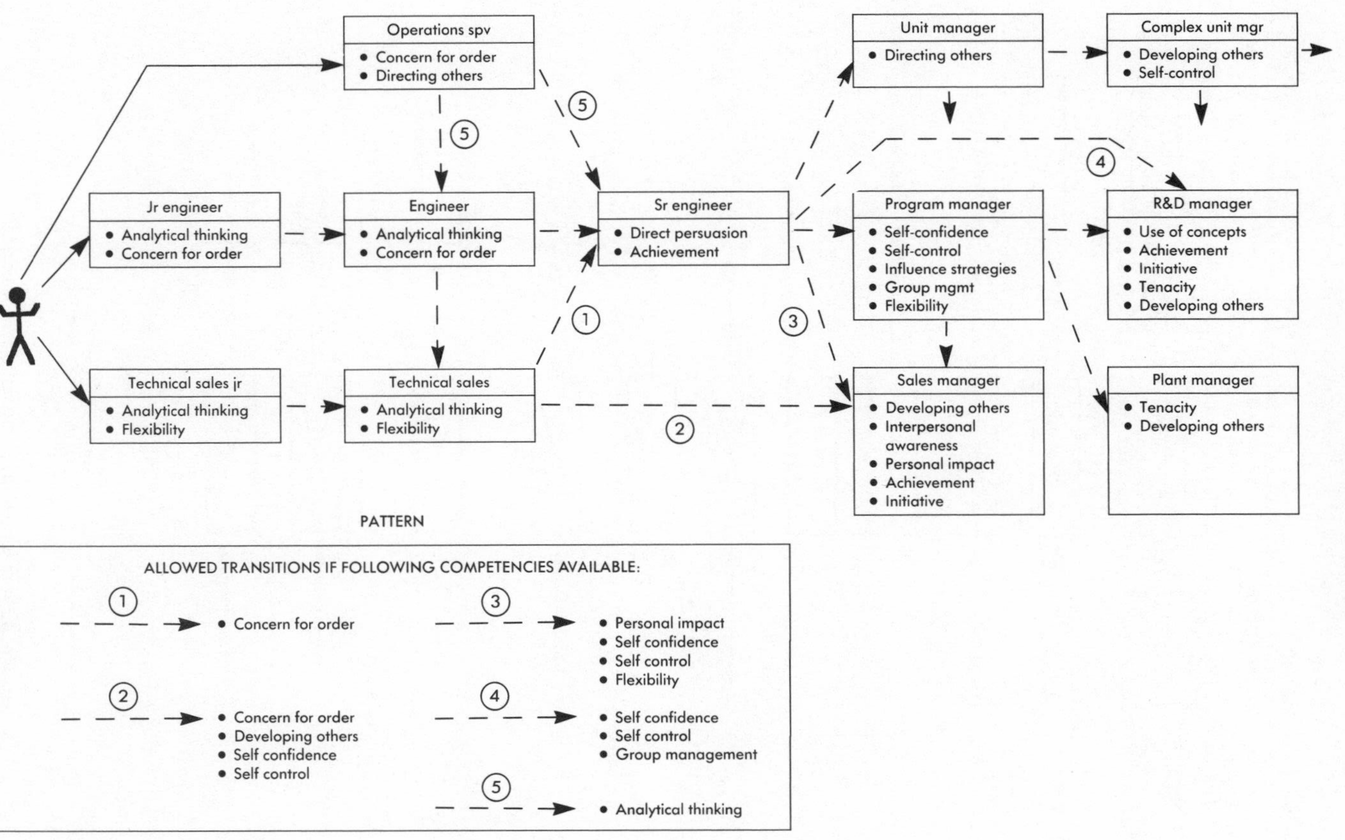

Figure 2.3 Key professional jobs career path in space telecommunication company

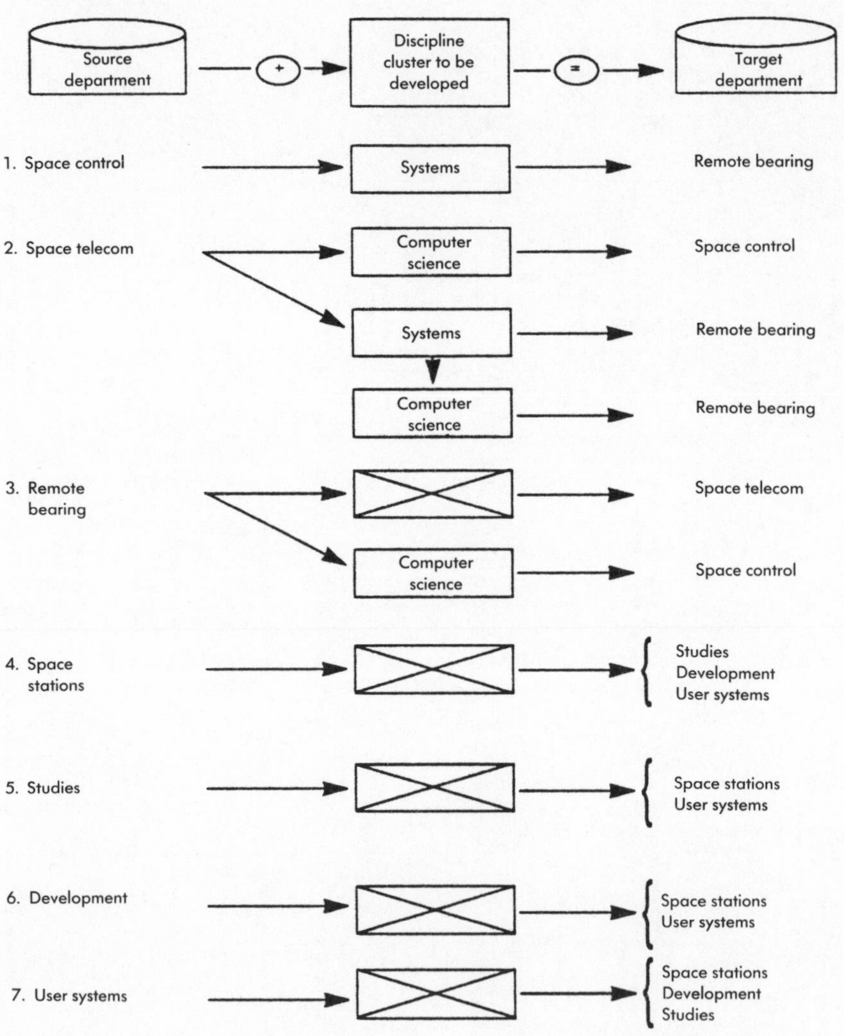

Figure 2.4 Framework of logical correspondence

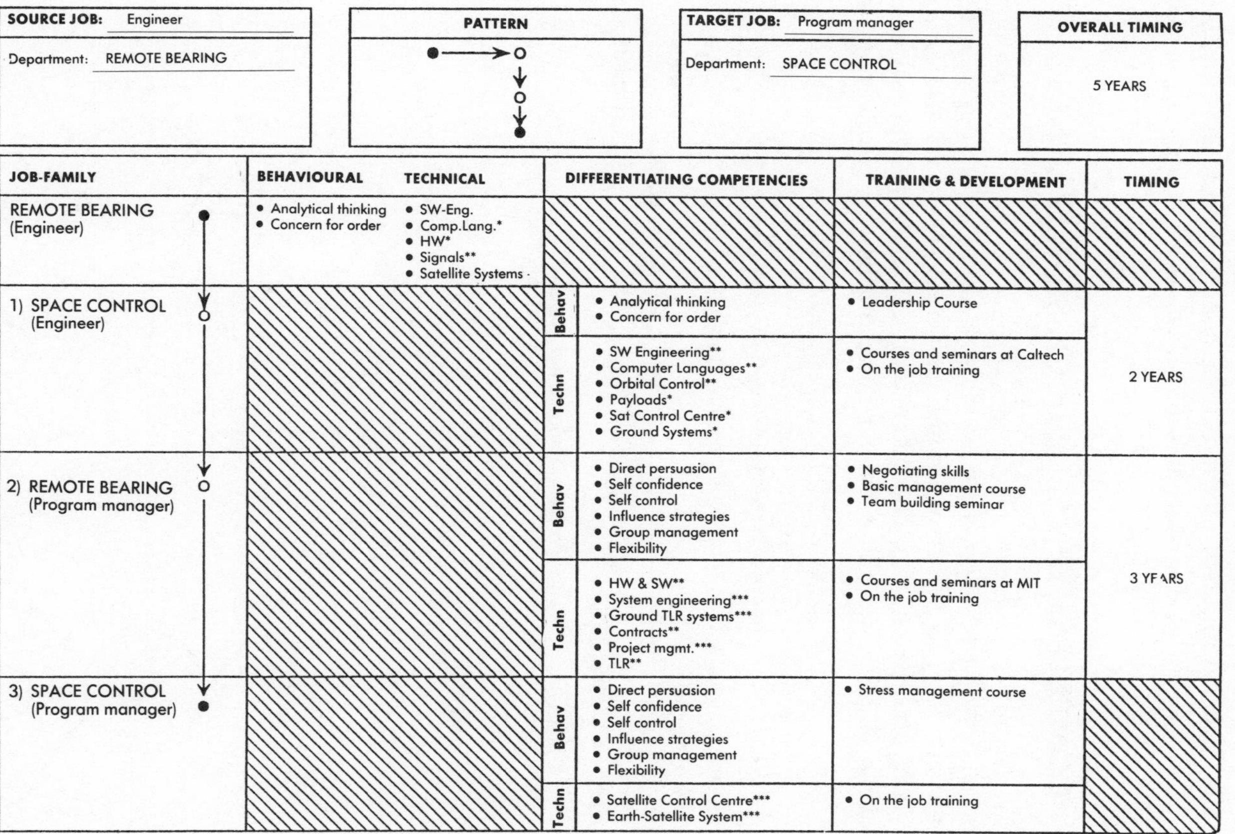

SOURCE JOB: Engineer	PATTERN	TARGET JOB: Program manager	OVERALL TIMING
Department: REMOTE BEARING	●——→○→○→●	Department: SPACE CONTROL	5 YEARS

JOB-FAMILY	BEHAVIOURAL	TECHNICAL		DIFFERENTIATING COMPETENCIES	TRAINING & DEVELOPMENT	TIMING
REMOTE BEARING (Engineer) ●	• Analytical thinking • Concern for order	• SW-Eng. • Comp.Lang.* • HW* • Signals** • Satellite Systems				
1) SPACE CONTROL (Engineer) ○			Behav	• Analytical thinking • Concern for order	• Leadership Course	2 YEARS
			Techn	• SW Engineering** • Computer Languages** • Orbital Control** • Payloads* • Sat Control Centre* • Ground Systems*	• Courses and seminars at Caltech • On the job training	
2) REMOTE BEARING (Program manager) ○			Behav	• Direct persuasion • Self confidence • Self control • Influence strategies • Group management • Flexibility	• Negotiating skills • Basic management course • Team building seminar	3 YEARS
			Techn	• HW & SW** • System engineering*** • Ground TLR systems*** • Contracts** • Project mgmt.*** • TLR**	• Courses and seminars at MIT • On the job training	
3) SPACE CONTROL (Program manager) ●			Behav	• Direct persuasion • Self confidence • Self control • Influence strategies • Group management • Flexibility	• Stress management course	
			Techn	• Satellite Control Centre*** • Earth-Satellite System***	• On the job training	

Figure 2.5 Job-family career path and development sheet

had to be programmed to drive people along the professional paths were defined both in the behavioural field and in the technical one (see Figure 2.5).

COMPETENCY-BASED SUCCESSION PLANNING

Competency-based succession planning enables an organisation to determine the critical current competencies necessary for success in key jobs and the strategic competencies necessary for future success (see Figure 2.6). Once this has determined the 'best fit' people, specific

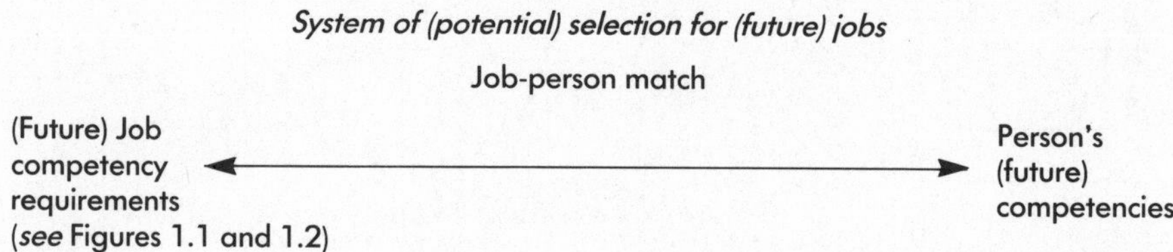

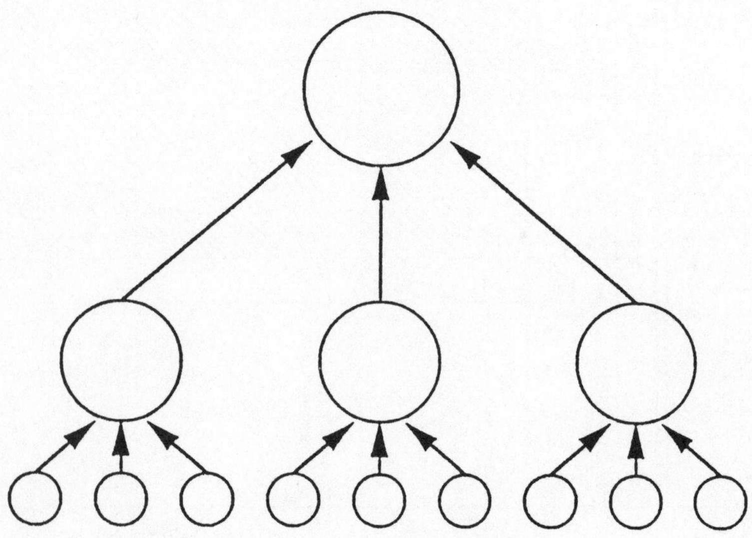

Figure 2.6 Succession planning

developmental plans can then be formulated that build upon these competency requirements to allow the individual's abilities to meet the strategic business needs of the organisation.

Results of succession planning

Many companies that have neglected management succession planning have suffered when key people leave unexpectedly. A recent joint study conducted by Hay with the University of Michigan and the Strategic Planning Institute[3] indicates that the existence of a formal succession plan for the top positions provides a measurable profit advantage to companies that implement those plans over those companies that do not. The profit advantage is even greater for firms that plan for succession of managers in the two layers below the top positions (see Figure 2.7). More extensive coverage of key resources shows greater emphasis on the strategic management of career paths and a strong link between promotion and performance. The results show up on the bottom line.

Links with career paths

Unlike replacement planning, management succession planning does not only identify high-potential candidates but also provides the organisation with a means of developing people who bear charcteristics that are critical to success. Such a system helps to ensure that the performance of these selected people will meet or exceed expectations when they are called upon to take up greater responsibility. The process assists top management in evaluating the gap between the candidate's current strengths, their developmental needs and the quality of skills required by the target job. This analysis allows for the candidate to be counselled in formulating an individual action plan to close this gap and tests the candidate's ability to progress in the career path.

Sometimes companies have difficulty in finding people for certain key jobs or retaining them once appointed. These companies often lack intermediate developmental steps between the feeder and target jobs, whereas the various job designs in the succession pattern require

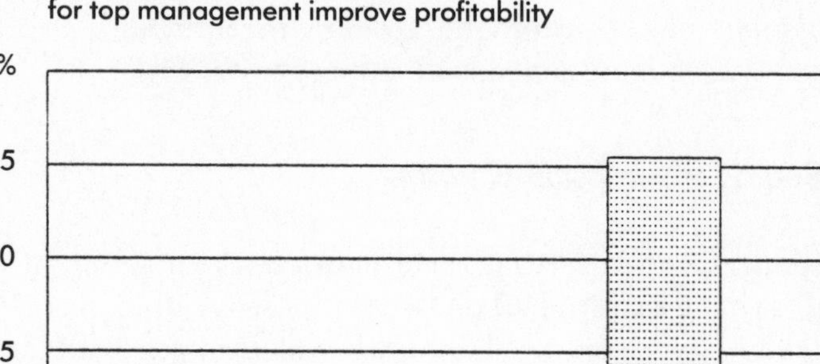

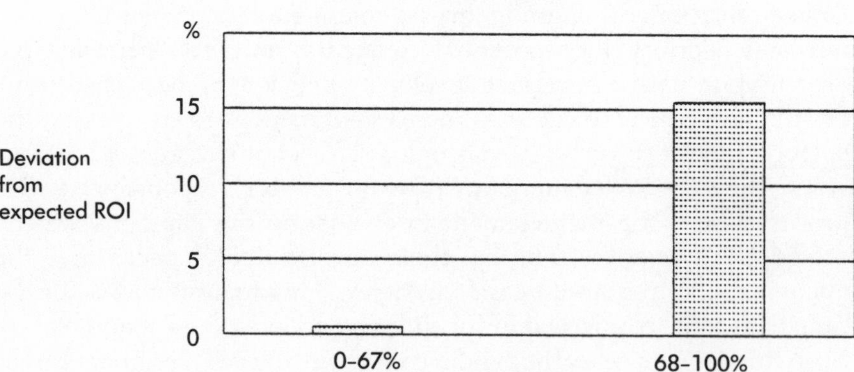

Figure 2.7 Succession planning and profitability

different skills, knowledge, traits or motives, which can be traced through the definition of competencies.

The accurate and systematic assessment of both the critical success factors required of either key professional or key managerial jobs and the evaluation and monitoring of the best person–job fit against these factors are the added value of using competency-based succession planning (Figure 2.8).

Steps to implement the system

For the competency-based succession planning to be complete, a logical process consisting of a certain number of steps must be followed. These key steps are as follows:

1. identify critical jobs that the organisation needs to fill;
2. develop a competency model from critical jobs, determining the competencies needed at each step of the job family ladder;
3. develop the most appropriate assessment methods (assessment centre, screening, interviewing, etc) and assess people against the competency model of the job;
4. make the decision whether to:
   - — promote from inside
     - now or
     - after competencies x, y, z have been developed;
   - — not promote but consider
     - possible lateral transfer;
     - keeping in current job or
     - deselection;
   - — recruit from outside if no one in the organisation is ready or can be developed in time;
5. feed the human resource management information system to track:
   - — promotable employees, for future competencies monitoring;
   - — competency requirements of target jobs;
6. develop succession planning hypothesis.

The outcome of this process is illustrated in Figure 2.9, which shows

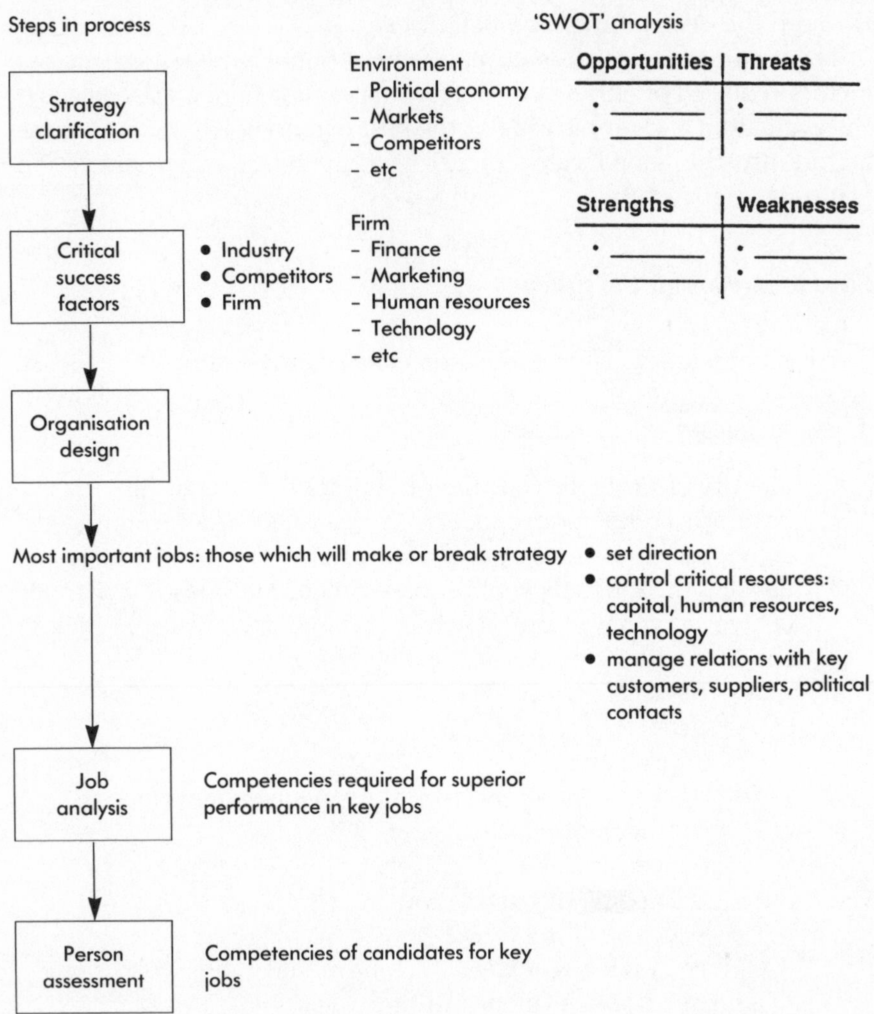

Figure 2.8 Top management succession planning

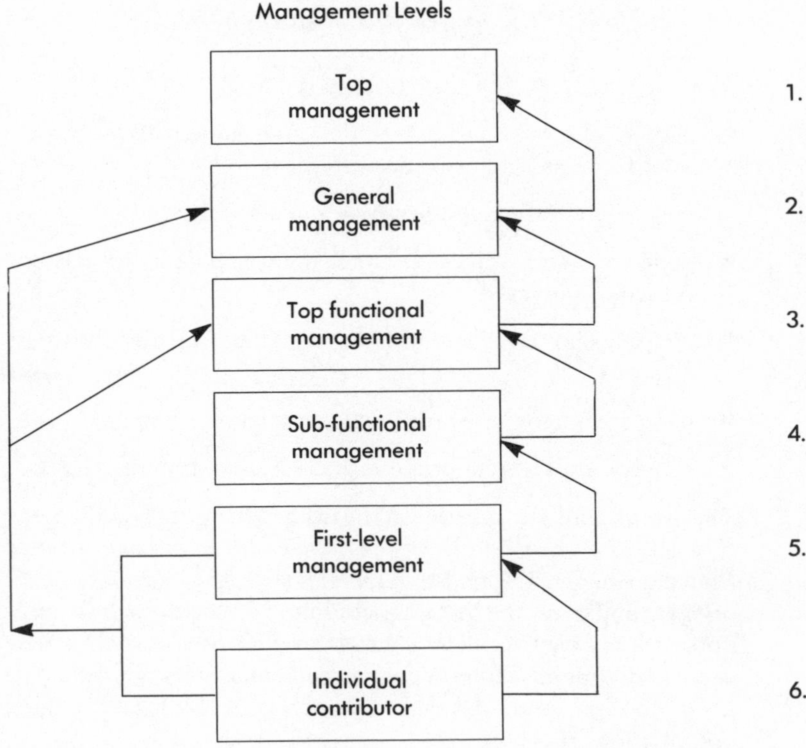

Source: Mahler, WR and Drotter, SJ (1986) *The Succession Planning Handbook for the Chief Executive* Mahler Publishing.

Figure 2.9 A succession planning data sheet

a possible way to represent the resulting succession list on a succession planning data sheet.

Case study of a succession planning exercise

The company is a regional insurance firm wanting to expand beyond being just a regional property and accident company, to develop new products and services to enhance market positioning, to enter strategic market alliances that would improve its market share and penetration.

Requirements of strategy

The implementation of this strategy required:

- people who are market-oriented and market-driven rather than technical and operations focused;
- people who can envisage new products and services;
- people who can effectively implement and generate positive returns on investments;
- people who can develop, manage and nurture business alliances;
- people who are innovative and can tolerate change;
- people who are goal-oriented and accomplishment driven.

These requirements resulted in the need to have managers able to translate the chief executive's strategies into concrete actions. Managers had to respond to high standards and expectations, to delegate and to escape being caught in the red tape of administration, to be willing to challenge the status quo and research for new ways to do things. The company needed managers who could be good models and develop leadership within a changing organisation.

Job competency assessment conducted on the basis of these requirements, using behavioural event interviews and expert panels, indicated that the competency profile to perform in the new environment demanded: initiative, self-confidence, achievement orientation, the ability to direct others, interpersonal sensitivity, group management skills and innovation.

The findings from the 11 executives' assessments (obtained using the focused interview technique) were examined to determine scores for the seven necessary executive competencies required to achieve the company's strategic goals.

Action to be taken

Figure 2.10 shows the final outcome, which led the chief executive to act as follows:

- invest in development of executives A, B, C, L and F, who would be key future players, in line with new needs;

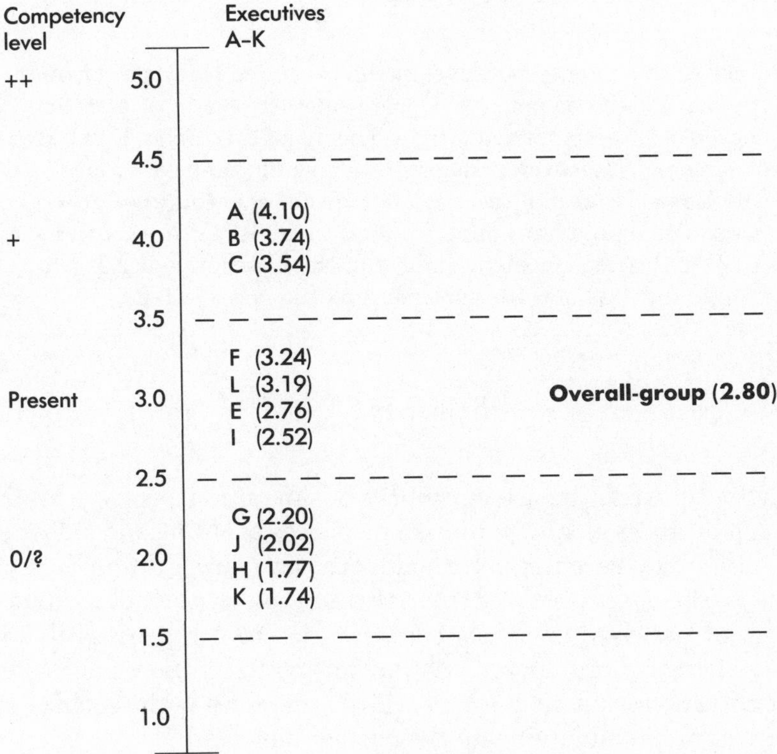

Figure 2.10 Insurance company executives' positioning versus overall strategic competencies

- formalise strategy to remove or replace executives, K, H, J and G;
- test for competencies in the next levels of management in the company;
- start replacement actions immediately, as this is critical to implementing the strategy and refocusing key players;
- re-think organisational structure *vis-à-vis* strategy, after answering some critical questions:
  — what is the right design?

— what are the accountabilities of strategic players?
— what are the specific competency profiles of the specific jobs?

Overall, the competency level of the executive team was below standard, high competency people being offset by low competency people, ie, competency drain. Too many executives, four out of eleven, demonstrated unacceptable overall competency levels. The lowest score for the executive group was found in group management and innovation - critical issues for future success.

After this management audit, the chief executive decided to change the deadlines for implementing the new strategy.

SUMMARY

As radical changes transform work, business and people, the link between business planning, human resources planning and individual career life-cycles becomes more and more necessary. Putting the right people in the right places at the right time must now allow for the process of matching available competencies to company goals in a rapidly changing framework. Within this context, the use of career paths and succession planning provides companies with flexible tools to attract, retain and motivate the people they need.

REFERENCES

1. Weick, KE (1977) 'Organisations as self-designing systems' *Organisational Dynamics*, vol 6, no 2.

2. Boyatzis RE (1982) *The Competent Manager* John Wiley and Sons

3. Unpublished paper produced in 1988 by The Hay Group, The Strategic Planning Institute and the University of Michigan.

3

Competency-based Recruitment and Selection

Charles E Bethell-Fox
Hay Group, UK

PRINCIPLES OF DESIGN

Selection systems, to be effective, must exhibit certain characteristics. First, they must successfully identify the person in the applicant pool who is best suited to take the job and provide the sort of job performance the organisation needs to gain its objectives. Second, this goal must be achieved without bias towards irrelevant characteristics such as gender, ethnicity, or irrelevant disability. Third, the operation of the selection system must be cost-effective so that the time and money spent on its design and administration is justified by the quality of the new recruits who are hired.

These goals can be readily achieved by the careful design and implementation of competency-based recruitment selection systems. By first carefully researching the competencies required for successful job performance, competency-based systems ensure that the characteristics sought during the selection process are those that will enable new job holders to deliver results. In addition, because the competencies identified are only those that affect actual job performance, the likelihood of bias based on selecting for irrelevant characteristics, such as gender or ethnicity, is much diminished. Furthermore, because carefully designed and implemented competency-based selection systems systems produce new job holders who deliver results, the benefits of implementing such systems far outweigh their costs.

This chapter is divided into three sections. The first outlines the best methods for identifying which competencies to include in the selection system. The second section provides recommendations regarding which methods to use in measuring these competencies in new job applicants. Finally, a means by which the quality of the process can be assured is decribed with practical recommendations.

SPECIFYING THE COMPETENCIES

Performance criteria

Before selecting a person for a job, the first step must be to decide what qualities to look for in the applicant. Traditionally, this has been done via a process called job analysis where the content of a job is studied in detail and the personal qualities needed to fill that role are inferred from the demands on the job holder. The weakness of this approach is that the inferred links, between what a job demands and the personal qualities that will supposedly enable a job holder to meet those demands, are typically based as much on faith and the experience of the job analyst as on any empirically demonstrable connections.

Furthermore, even when the personal qualities identified by the analyst are the right ones, it is very difficult, just by looking at job content alone, to identify which of the qualities listed are particularly important in producing superior as opposed to merely acceptable job performance. Hay/McBer has put considerable time and effort into developing a more effective technique for identifying the personal qualities needed for jobs. This method begins not by focusing on the content of the job, but rather by specifying clearly what it is that the job should deliver as output. In other words, the method takes as its starting point job *performance* rather than job *content*. So, the first step is for the organisation to examine the position to be filled and answer a simple question: 'What are the performance criteria for the new job holder that we would use in deciding whether or not we had hired the right person?'

In a production job the main criterion might be 'Produce X amount of product Y to quality standard Z, by time T'. In a service job 'Provide effective answers/solutions to clients' needs/problems promptly and courteously'. In a sales job 'Sell X amount of product Y by time T with few customer complaints and high levels of repeat business'. And for managers, whether of production, sales or service 'Manage a group of people who achieve productivity level X to quality standard Z by time T', as well as some planning and strategic outputs at more senior managerial levels.

Answering the above questions often requires some discussion, but the time consumed is time well spent. If the organisation does not have a clear view of what it is looking for from its employees in terms of performance, then there is no clear goal to shoot for when trying to find new people who are capable of delivering the type of performance that will help the organisation achieve its objectives.

There are several ways to get a clear picture of the performance criteria required by a job. Probably the most efficient approach is to call a meeting (known as an expert panel; see also Chapter 1) with people in the organisation who hold jobs senior to the position in question and/or with people who depend, for their own effectiveness, on the outputs from the job concerned. The meeting is used to place the job in the context of the larger organistion and to understand what the major outputs from the job must be, as well as how these outputs relate to other members of the organisation fulfilling their roles. These 'outputs' refer not only to productivity levels but also to quality standards, behaviours and so on.

With a straightforward picture of what aspects of performance in the job are valued by the organisation, candidates can be selected who not only are capable of filling a job, but also of delivering the high levels of performance that will help the organisation achieve its objectives. Organisations that contain these high performers are not only more likely to achieve organisational goals, but also are more likely to generate the sort of stimulating work environments that lead to greater job satisfaction for all job holders.

Having got a clear fix on the key performance criteria for the job, the next step in the Hay/McBer methodology is to identify the personal qualities to look for in new job applicants that will enable them to deliver the levels of performance needed by the organisation.

Selection competencies for superior performance

When a job currently exists within an organisation, it is usually possible to identify a group of existing job holders who, for whatever reason, already deliver at least some aspects of the superior levels of performance specified as desirable by the expert panel. Indeed, a large body of research shows that individual differences in job performance are very substantial across most jobs. For example, Hunter, Schmidt and Judiesch, integrating the results of 81 independent research investigations, found that, on average, in blue collar and routine clerical jobs superior performers (the top 15 per cent of job holders) deliver at least 19 per cent more than average job holders, with performance differences rising to 47 per cent and 120 per cent in professional and sales jobs respectively.[1]

Once the expert panel has reached a consensus regarding the performance criteria for a job, current job holders who already exemplify at least some of the performance characteristics sought for the new job can be identified without too much difficulty. The panel can also usually find a group of current job holders whose performance is adequate but not superior. Working with these two groups of superior and average performers the job analyst can now identify the personal characteristics, traits, skills and abilities (collectively known as competencies) that give rise not just to acceptable but to superior job performance and which should, therefore, be sought in the selection of new job holders.

The best way for the job analyst to do this is via behavioural event interviews (see also Chapter 2). This technique involves interviewing each average and each superior job holder to obtain a detailed account of the thoughts, actions and interactions that have enabled each individual to achieve specific performance-related outcomes in the job. The transcripts from these interviews are then carefully coded for the personal traits, characteristics and skills that each interviewee exhibits. Those traits and skills which appear in the transcripts of average as well as superior job performers constitute the essential competency requirements of the job. However, the data also provide a powerful means for identifying the competencies that differentiate superior from average job holders: those traits and skills that are unique to, or that appear with higher frequency, in the transcripts of the superior performers represent the competencies that drive superior performance. The process of selecting new job applicants is then quite straightforward. If, in the selection process, we identify applicants who possess the essential competencies, as well as the competencies that differentiate superior job holders, then these new job holders will be able to perform the job satisfactorily and deliver superior performance.

The behavioural event interview is the most powerful modern technique available to identify the competencies associated with superior performance. By carefully defining what aspects of job output and performance will be important now as well as in the future, the expert panel can identify those aspects of performance which the organisation believes it will particularly need in the future.

Sometimes it may not be possible to conduct behavioural event interviews with current job holders. In these circumstances there are other means available to identify the competencies to look for in the selection process. One of the more popular alternative methods is described below.

Generic selection competencies

If the job for which applicants must be selected is a new position or current job holders are not available for behavioural event interviewing, then the results of an accumulated knowledge base of competencies can be exploited to begin to sketch out the likely competencies that should be sought in the selection process. By applying the behavioural event interviewing technique over the lat 20 years in a wide range of jobs and organisations throughout the world, Hay/McBer has found that at least some competencies recur frequently across different jobs. In particular, some 20 generic competencies appear to give rise to at least some aspects of superior job performance across a range of entrepreneurial, technical, professional, sales, service and managerial roles. These fall into six main groups of competencies:

1. Achievement and action competencies:
   - achievement motivation: a concern for working well or competing against a standard of excellence;
   - concern for order and quality: a concern to reduce

uncertainty by monitoring and checking and setting up clear and orderly systems;
- initiative: a predisposition to take action, to improve results or create opportunities;
- information seeking: curiosity and the desire to acquire broad as well as specific information to get to the bottom of issues.

2. Helping and service competencies:
   - interpersonal understanding: the ability accurately to hear and understand and respond to the unspoken or partly expressed thoughts, feelings or concerns of others;
   - customer service orientation: a desire to help or serve others by discovering and then meeting their needs. 'Customers' may include internal colleagues.
3. Influencing competencies
   - impact and influence: a desire to have a specific impact or effect on others, to persuade, convince, influence or impress others to get them to go along with an agenda or course of action;
   - organisational awareness: the ability to understand and use the political dynamics within organisations;
   - relationship building: the ability to build and maintain friendly contacts with people who are or will be useful in achieving work-related goals.
4. Managerial competencies
   - developing others: an ability to take effective action to improve others' skills and talents;
   - directiveness: an ability to tell others what needs to be done and to make others comply with one's wishes with the long term good of the organisation in mind;
   - teamwork and co-operation: the ability to work and to get others to work co-operatively with others;
   - team leadership: the ability to take a role as leader of a team or group.
5. Cognitive competencies
   - analytical thinking: the ability to understand situations and solve problems by breaking them down into their

constituent pieces and thinking about them in a systematic and logical way;

— conceptual thinking: the ability to identify patterns or connections between situations and key or underlying issues in complex situations;

— expertise: the ability to use and expand technical knowledge or to distribute work-related knowledge to others.

6. Personal effectiveness competencies

— self-control: the ability to maintain self-control when faced with emotion-provoking or stressful situations;

— self-confidence: a belief in one's ability to select an appropriate approach to, and to accomplish, a task, especially in challenging circumstances;

— flexibility: the ability to adapt to and work effectively within a variety of situations and with various individuals and groups;

— organisational commitment: the ability and willingness to align one's own behaviour with the needs, priorities and goals of the organisation.

In any one particular job only a subset of this generic list is important. Furthermore, the list is unlikely to include *all* the competencies important for superior performance in any specific job. Therefore, behavioural event interviews should always be conducted whenever existing superior job holders are available.

For selection as well as other purposes, each of these generic competencies has been organised into an ascending scale of behavioural indicators of each competency. The ordering of the behavioural indicators on each scale is based on the intensity of action, impact, complexity and time horizon of each indicator, as observed in transcripts from Hay/McBer's database of behavioural event interview transcripts containing instances of the competency. For example, our analysis of the generic competency achievement motivation, across a range of behavioural event interview studies, reveals eight generic indicators of its presence which can be organised into the ascending scale.

1. Tries to do job well: may express frustration at waste or inefficiency (eg gripes about wasted time and wants to do

better) but does not cause specific improvements;
2. works to meet a standard set by management (eg manages to a budget, meets sales quotas);
3. creates own measures of excellence to measure outcomes against a standard of excellence not imposed by management;
4. makes specific changes in the system or in own work methods to improve performance (eg does something better, faster, at lower cost, more efficiently; improves quality, customer satisfaction, morale, revenues), without setting any specific goal;
5. sets challenging goals, ie there is about a 50–50 chance of actually achieving the goal, or refers to specific measures of baseline performance compared with better performance at a later point in time: eg, 'When I took over, efficiency was 20 per cent – now it is up to 85 per cent';
6. makes cost-benefit analyses, makes decisions, sets priorities or chooses goals on the basis of inputs and outputs; makes explicit considerations of potential profit, return on investment or cost-benefit analysis;
7. takes calculated entrepreneurial risks and commits significant resources and/or time (in the face of uncertainty) to improve performance, tries something new, reaches a challenging goal, while also taking action to minimise the risk involved, or encourages and supports subordinates in taking entrepreneurial risks;
8. persists in entrepreneurial efforts and takes numerous, sustained actions over time in the face of obstacles to reach entrepreneurial goals, or successfully completes entrepreneurial endeavours.

These rank orderings of competency indicators are known as 'just noticeable difference scales'. In moving from one level to the next the associated incremental change in behaviour should be sufficiently distinct to allow the change to be readily observable and measurable, otherwise, the scale is likely to be of little value in an applied measurement context. It is also possible to construct just noticeable difference scales for competencies which are relatively unique to a specific job based on data from the behavioural event interviews.

Once a consensus on the general performance criteria required for a job has been achieved, the expert panel inspects the definition and the just noticeable difference scale associated with each generic competency and rates:

- the importance of the competency to overall effectiveness in the job;
- the level on the scale that is most descriptive of minimally acceptable job performance;
- the level that is most descriptive of the superior level of performance that can reasonably be expected from job holders.

The expert panel capitalises on its knowledge of the job to identify the generic competencies that are likely to be important in the job and to provide a profile of the levels required for acceptable and superior performance across competencies. This profile provides a template for the competencies and competency levels to search for in the selection process.

A selection competency template based on these ratings is somewhat subjective, although the accuracy of the template can be enhanced by ensuring that the expert panel discusses each rating in detail. Consequently, to ensure objectivity and accuracy in the design of the selection competency template, whenever possible behavioural event interviews with actual job holders should be the method of choice.

Simplifying the selection competency template

The selection competency template should contain as few competencies as possible. Typically, a careful analysis will show that six or seven competencies support the key components of job performance and account for most of the differences between average and superior performers. These are the competencies that should form the prime focus of the selection system. The number of competencies in the selection template can also be kept to manageable proportions by deciding which competencies can be trained rather than selected for.

Some competencies take longer to train or develop than others. For example 'achievement motivation' and other motive competencies start to develop in the very earliest years of people's lives and usually change only slowly in adulthood. On the other hand, skill-based competencies, such as computer programing or financial management skills can be acquired relatively quickly at any time in a person's working life. Therefore, while successful efforts can be made to train motive competencies[2] it is usually more practical to select for motive as well as deeply rooted trait-based competencies. If the deeply rooted competencies required for superior performance in a particular job, such as achievement motivation interpersonal understanding, impact and influence and self-confidence can be identified in a job applicant but some of the easily trained, skill-based competencies are missing, then it usually makes sense to hire the applicant. However, if the converse is true, a job offer should probably not be made because, while the skill-based competencies may be present, the applicant lacks the deeper personal qualities that will give rise to superior performance in the longer term. Hence, those competencies that the organisation can easily afford to train should be removed from the selection template.

Ensuring credibility of selection competency template

If the selection process is to be run by the organisation's own staff, then not only must the template be accurate but also the organisation's staff must see it as accurate and credible. Otherwise, selection staff are unlikely to make use of the template during selection. The best way to ensure credibility is to take excerpts from the behavioural event interview transcripts that provide vivid examples of each competency in action on the job and illustrate how each competency in the template drives successful job performance. In those instances where no behavioural event interview data is available, then the expert panel must be carefully staffed not only with those who have detailed knowledge of the job in question but also who have credibility within the organisation.

MEASURING SELECTION COMPETENCIES IN JOB APPLICANTS

Advertising

New job applicants may come from inside or outside the organisation. In either case, once the selection competency template has been specified, the first step must be to encourage the right sort of applicants to apply for the job. This means that, whether advertising is done inside or outside the organisation, the advertisement should contain accurate information about the nature of the job and the competencies sought. This allows potential applicants to make an informed initial decision about whether the job is likely to provide a sufficient match to their competencies to allow them to perform well and to derive satisfaction from the work entailed.

If the job requires a strong analytical thinker, with high achievement motivation and the ability to acquire technical information quickly, coupled with strong influencing skills and the desire to respond to the needs of demanding customers, then the advertisement should say so. Using the advertisement primarily to try to sell the job is unlikely to benefit anyone. The most likely consequence is too many unsuitable applicants, who will have to be weeded out at substantial cost in the subsequent selection process. It is far more effective to view the advertisement as the first stage in the selection process where applicants begin the process by selecting themselves for jobs. They can only hope to do this effectively if they are supplied with accurate information about the job and the competencies demanded. Given a suitable pool of applicants, the next step is to conduct a preliminary sift of this pool to identify which applicants should be invited for interview.

Biodata and the design of application forms

The application form for a job vacancy can be specifically designed to begin the process of measuring relevant competencies in job applicants. For example, an entry-level managerial job may require competencies such as team leadership and directiveness and, perhaps, developing others. Biographical information about a candidate's past experiences (biodata) taken from application forms can be used, with some degree of predictive accuracy, to form preliminary assessments of candidates' likely competencies.

For example, applicants whose past working or leisure experiences involve them in developing others' skills (eg, having responsibility for others from a position of authority) or in team leadership (eg, captaincy in team sports) may be more likely to have developed the competencies necessary for the job than those applicants who lack such experiences. Similarly, if the job requires strong achievement motivation then a past record of high achievement in different areas of work is probably a positive indicator. The competencies measured through biodata can be quite specific. For example, in a study of executives sent to foreign countries, demanding an 'overseas adjustment' competency[3], it was found that those job holders who were more successful were more likely to have travelled voluntarily when young and to have learned to speak a foreign language.

The examination of biodata on application forms can be systematised to such an extent that a numerical biodata score can be derived for each applicant, which can then be used to predict future job success[4]. Application forms should be designed which systematically collect relevant biographical information about candidates. Biodata scores can then be computed as an aid to deciding which applicants should go forward to the next stage in the selection process.

Behavioural description indices and competency assessment questionnaires

Candidates can also supply preliminary information about their competencies by rating their own behaviours on behavioural description indices.

These can be designed to measure all 20 generic selection competencies or they can be instruments tailored to measure competencies specific to a particular job. For example, if the selection competency template indicates that influence and impact is one of the keys to superior performance, job applicants can be asked to rate the accuracy of self-descriptive statements such as:

- I try to identify other's issues and concerns before presenting my position;

- I can usually persuade people to see things my way;
- I am good at supporting my ideas with relevant facts and information;
- I often use more than one approach when I want to convince someone of something.

Other questions that help to assess how frankly and openly each job applicant answers such questions can be included on such indices. For example, if a candidate strongly disagrees with statements such as

- sometimes I make mistakes in social behaviour;
- sometimes I am lazy;
- sometimes I am envious of other people;

then it is unlikely that the candidate is providing an accurate self-description and so the answers to all the other questions on the index must be interpreted with caution. Provided that candidates appear to be providing frank and open self-assessment, a total score on each competency can be computed by summing up all the ratings across relevant questions.

For job applicants who are already working for the organisation, ratings of each applicant's competencies can also be collected via '360-degree' assessments using competency assessment questionnaires. Here managers, peers and subordinates can rate, based on their observations of the candidates in the workplace, how often the candidate exhibits the behaviours associated with particular competencies in appropriate circumstances. So if, for example, the candidate's managers, peers and subordinates agree that the candidate:

- gives people assignments or training to develop their abilities;
- gives others specific detailed feedback on their performance;
- gives encouragement to others to improve their motivation;
- devotes significant time to providing task related help to others;

then the implication is that, to a significant degree, the candidate possesses a high level of the developing others' competency.

Scores from behavioural description indices and competency

assessment questionnaires can be compared to normative tables and the competency requirements for a job and used, with biodata, to form a preliminary assessment of each candidate's strengths and weaknesses. Such scores can also be used to decide which candidates should be invited forward for interview.

Interviews

The next stage in the selection process is the interview. Here, a specific type of structured interview has been developed that directly assesses the competencies possessed by applicants that appear in the selection template for a job. Known as the focused interview, this technique asks candidates to describe in detail relevant experiences in their past. Through a structured probing technique, the interviewer searches for evidence that during the experience the candidate exhibited the behaviours associated with any of the selection competencies. For example, to search for behaviours associated with achievement motivation, a candidate might be asked to describe an experience where 'you achieved something on your own'. Focused interviewing can be easily learned, with a little practice, even by people who have had no prior experience of selection methods.

Focused interviewing is highly effective both in terms of predictive accuracy and cost-effectiveness. For example, in one study[5] 33 sales people were hired using focused interviewing based on a competency template. A further 41 were selected using traditional methods. A careful follow-up of the study revealed that, on an annual basis, competency-selected salespeople each sold, on average, Ecu 71,000 more per year than the other group.

Tests

A wide range of different psychological tests can also be used to support the interviewing process, including cognitive ability tests and personality questionnaires. Cognitive ability tests can be used to measure particular aspects of the cognitive competencies, such as analytical thinking, as well as general cognitive ability. It is, however, important that any tests used should be relevant to the competencies in the selection template. For example, scores on a test that requires test takers to identify effective arguments may not necessarily predict a candidate's ability to *make* effective arguments in writing or in presentations on the job. Tests that closely simulate actual job demands are likely to be the most effective. Personality questionnaires that provide self-assessments of a variety of different competencies and scores from these measures, like those from behavioural description indices and competency assessment questionnaires, can usefully be compared with normative tables for particular job applicant groups.

Simulations, practical exercises and assessment centres

Practical simulations and exercises add great value to virtually any selection process. They are designed to simulate as closely as possible the competency demands of the post. For example, if the job requires teamwork and co-operation then a group discussion or practical exercise can be designed that requires several candidates to work together to reach an agreement or to achieve some other team-related goal. If the job requires customer service orientation, then a role play exercise can be designed where each candidate deals with a complaining customer played by an actor. If the job requires paperwork then an in-tray exercise can be constructed that simulates appropriate job demands. Critical job-related situations, observed during behavioural event interviews, can provide powerful data to aid in the design of such exercises. Trained assessors observe the behaviours shown or the documents produced by candidates during these exercises and assess the levels of competency demonstrated.

These exercises are often grouped together with interviews and tests in selection processes known as assessment centres, which may take a day or more to administer to each group of half a dozen or so candidates. While full-blown assessment centres take time to administer, they provide the most sophisticated means available to assess candidates' competencies from a variety of different perspectives. However, when time is short and an assessment centre is not a viable option, then a careful examination of each candidate's background information or biodata, followed by a thorough focused interview, usually constitute the best way of getting an all round assessment of each candidate's competencies in the shortest possible time.

Comparing applicants' competencies to job requirements

The just noticeable difference scales used to specify the selection competency template for a job can also be used as a means of recording each candidate's level on each competency, as assessed by any of these measurement techniques. In this way, a direct visual comparison can be made between a candidate's assessed competency profile and the competency levels required for superior performance in the job. The difference between the two profiles is a direct measure of how well the candidate is suited to the job and, therefore, also a measure of how likely the candidate is to deliver superior performance in that job.

A visual comparison of the two profiles is usually sufficient to inform any selection decision but, if there are many applicants or possible candidates for a job, then a computer can help in finding which candidate profile provides the closest match to the job's competency requirements. For example, the computer can be used to calculate the average difference between the assessed and the required level of each competency for each candidate and then to rank candidates according to the size of this difference.

QUALITY ASSURANCE

Installing a competency-based recruitment and selection system is only the first implementation step. To ensure that the system is operating properly, follow-up and monitoring are essential. There are three practical follow-up steps that should be taken to ensure that the system is delivering superior job performers, fairly and cost-effectively.

Predictive value

Once the selection system has been operating for a few months, the job performance of those hired through it should be carefully examined to ensure that the new recruits are delivering the results needed. One way to do this is to compare the performance of those identified by the selection system as truly outstanding candidates with the performance of those who were predicted by the system to be capable of delivering good but not superior performance. Alternatively, the job performance of a group of job holders hired via the organisation's traditional selection methods can be compared with the performance delivered by those hired through competency-based methods. If the competency-based selection methods have been installed properly then the predictive power of the new system should be strong. Follow-ups of this sort, in past studies, have shown performance improvements ranging from 19 per cent to 78 per cent as a result of using competency-based selection methods. Reductions in employee turnover ranging from 50 per cent to 90 per cent have also been noted[6].

Fairness

The best way to ensure that the selection system is operating fairly is to collect information systematically on items such as candidates' gender, ethnicity and disabilities and then to monitor whether success at selection is correlated with individual characteristics that should not affect the selection decision. If any correlations are found the source of the bias should be isolated and remedial action taken. Not surprisingly, competency-based selection systems tend to be fairer than selection systems based on irrelevant personal characteristics. For example, in one study in the retail sector, traditional selection methods were found to give rise to the disproportionate hiring of white males. Introducing a competency-based selection system resulted in the hiring of more women and ethnic minorities[7].

Cost-effectiveness

For most jobs it is possible to calculate the monetary value associated with superior job performance. Depending on the complexity of the job, it is not unusual for superior performers to deliver one-and-a-half to two times more, in terms of bottom line results, than average performers. The costs of installing a competency-based selection system are quickly outweighed by the benefits that accrue. For example, Spencer (1986) reports a return on investment from one competency-based selection programme of 2,300 per cent: the monetary value of improved performance and retention as a result of using the selection system in just its first year of operation outweighed the costs of installing the system by 23:1. Cost benefit analyses of this type should be conducted wherever possible to demonstrate unambiguously that the selection system is worth the time and the energy that the organisation devotes to it.

SUMMARY

Effective selection systems identify the competencies associated with high performance, establish assessment techniques that successfully measure the presence of competencies in candidates, and repay their own expense through the additional productivity of new recruits. Suitably validated to confirm the appropriateness of competency requirements for performance, and the absence of irrelevant bias, selection systems represent a key area of competitive advantage.

REFERENCES

1. Hunter, JE, Schmidt, FL and Judiesch, MK (1990) 'Individual differences in output variability as a function of job complexity' *Journal of Applied Psychology* 75(1) pp 28–42.
2. McClelland, DC (1987) *Human Motivation* Cambridge University Press.
3. Mansfield, RS and Mumford, S 'A competency-based approach to intercultural relations' in Mansfield, RS (1982) *Advanced Intercultural Relations Workshop Design* McBer and Company, Boston MA.
4. Hunter, JE and Hunter, RF (1984) 'Validity and utility of alternative predictors of job performance' *Psychological Bulletin* 96, pp 72–98.
5. Buchhorn, D (1991) 'Behavioural Event Interview Quantitative Results' L'Oreal Corporation, New York.
6. Spencer, LM, McClelland, DC and Spencer, SM (1992) *Competency Assessment Methods: History and State of the Art* Hay/McBer Research Press.
7. Spencer, LM (1986) *Calculating Human Resource Costs and Benefits* John Wiley & Sons.

4

Potential Analysis in Management Development

Manfred Strombach
Hay, Germany

All organisations make a range of decisions about their managers. They need to determine whom to select, dismiss, promote and develop. To make sound decisions, organisations need to assess their managers by appraising their current performance and assessing their future potential. Within the general framework of the preceding chapter, this article focuses on the area of potential assessment. The procedure, tools and results presented describe one example of a way of implementing a potential assessment system.

Hay's German consultancy practice has surveyed the methods European organisations use to analyse potential. Current practices include:

- unstructured methods, where the manager's superior typically assesses their subordinates' future potential subjectively;
- semi-structured methods, where the manager's superior and/or human resource specialists explore the relevant aspects of the subordinates' present performance to predict future potential;
- structured methods, where the manager's superior and human resource specialists use a combination of techniques, such as

assessment centres, psychometric questionnaires, interviews and appraisal data to establish the suitability of the subordinate against superior performer competencies in the target role(s).

This chapter describes how a structured approach was used within a German organisation to assess potential. The approach relates competency-based criteria as defined in previous chapters, to job evaluation criteria. This method is of particular relevance to organisations that have undertaken a managerial job evaluation exercise and wish to use this data to define job requirement criteria as an input to strategic management development. The steps taken provide an organisation with a means of comparing managerial potential with different jobs. The results can be used in succession planning, personal development and salary determination.

AIMS OF THE POTENTIAL ANALYSIS EXERCISE

The organisation concerned wished to assess the potential of managers between the ages of 30 to 45. It was important that the following criteria were met:

- the managers in question were not to be physically present during the assessment process;
- the managers' direct superiors and peers of superiors should contribute to the assessment;
- the time and effort needed to assess potential should not be too great for those involved;
- the time and effort needed to update the results should not be too great for the human resource team;
- the results of the potential assessment had to be presented in a meaningful manner so that the board of directors, superiors and human resource manager could make the required decisions and take action;
- the potential assessment system had to be capable of being maintained by the organisation itself.

Based upon these criteria a six-stage exercise was carried out.

Step 1: Preparation of job requirement criteria

The jobs within the organisation had already been reviewed as part of a job evaluation exercise and job descriptions were available for all the management population. These job descriptions were analysed to produce job requirement criteria by identifying the skills, situation specific criteria and competencies necessary for job holders. Job skills covered the technical know-how required for each particular job eg: engineering expertise and computer literacy. Situation specific criteria included freedom to think and act. Competencies addressed areas such as management know-how, eg: ability to plan and organise, develop others.

The competencies were described in terms of behaviours that distinguished outstanding performers from the rest and were clarified using a dictionary of competencies. These, together with skill and situation specific criteria, were aggregated to describe the requirements that each job needed and that job holders should meet. Each criterion was defined in terms that were meaningful to the organisation and the particular job under consideration, as shown in Table 4.1.

Step 2: Development of job requirement profiles

Superiors were presented with job requirement criteria for each of the jobs for which they were directly responsible. The requirement profile criteria levels for each position were determined using a scale from 0 to 5: the higher the level, the more important the criterion for superior performance in the defined role. If, for example, under the broad heading of managerial know-how, developing others was a high priority, this competency would be assigned a 4 or 5. Criteria each had detailed behavioural or technical definitions appropriate to the particular job role and organisational culture. The scales were also carefully defined so that superiors understood the difference between the various numerical levels.

The procedure was repeated to assign levels to each job requirement, to produce a requirement profile for the particular job under consideration. These profiles form the foundation for Step 3.

On the basis of these descriptions, a job requirement matrix could be prepared for each function within the management hierarchy. The

Table 4.1 Job requirement criteria

Type	Evaluation factor	Skill and competency (examples)
Technical know-how	Technical know-how	Research know-how Computer literacy
Competency	Management breadth	Team leadership Planning Organising Achievement motivation
	Human relations	Developing others Interpersonal understanding Impact and influence
	Thinking challenge	Analytical thinking Pattern recognition
Situation specific	Freedom to think Freedom to act Role impact	

profile for the job of section manager: research, for instance, had the requirements shown in Figure 4.1.

Step 3: Potential assessment interviews with superiors

The purpose of the potential assessment interviews with superiors was to compare the individual's personal profile with the relevant job requirement profile(s). In terms of person–job fit, it can be just as harmful to have too much as too little achievement motivation for a given job. Either could lead to an individual's inability to be a superior performer.

To assist with the potential assessment interview an interview reference book was prepared, containing standardised questions on the recruitment criteria. Areas such as management know-how were broken down into relevant competencies. The questions concerned

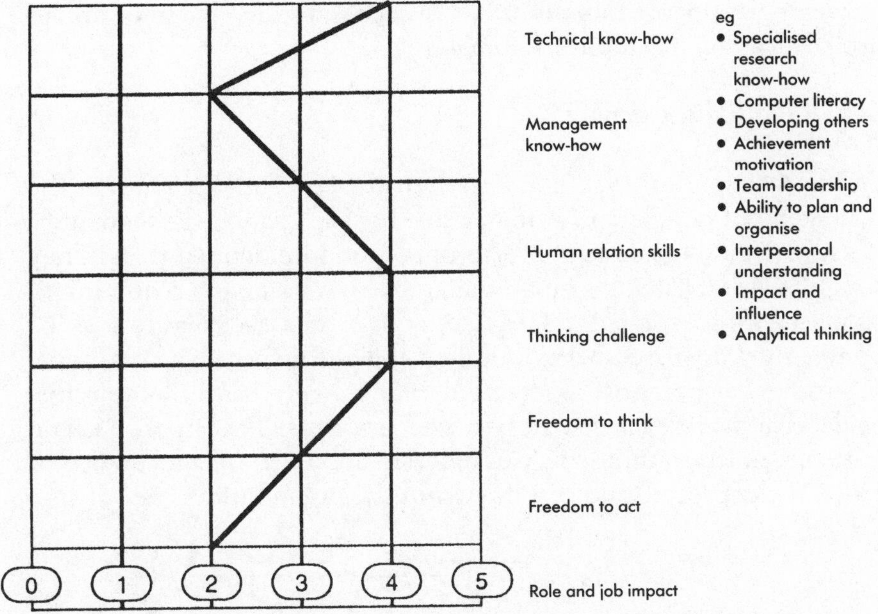

Note: The level assigned to technical know-how, management know-how and human relation skills represents a summary level for a cluster of job specific technical skills/competencies.

Figure 4.1 Job requirements for section manager: research

with management know-how covered the relevant competencies from the generic list referred to in Chapter 3.

Examples of questions concerning one criterion, developing others were:

- What tasks does he/she delegate?
- How frequently does he/she have development discussions with team members?
- What personal development plans are in place for each team member?
- What individual development has taken place for each team member during the last six months?

The superiors were asked to provide examples of behavioural

incidents to support their answers to each question. These examples provided a valuable input to Step 4.

Step 4: Panel discussions

Groups of superiors met to discuss individual potential profiles for the management population. A major role for each panel was to identify the most suitable managers for progression into defined roles. They sought to establish job–person match by comparing job requirement profiles with person potential assessment profiles (see Figure 4.2). To do this they discussed behavioural examples for the relevant criteria, ensuring that potential assessment ratings were based on objective evidence and were consistent between assessors. This cross checking mechanism led to uniformity of assessment standards and an acceptance of the process and results within the organisation.

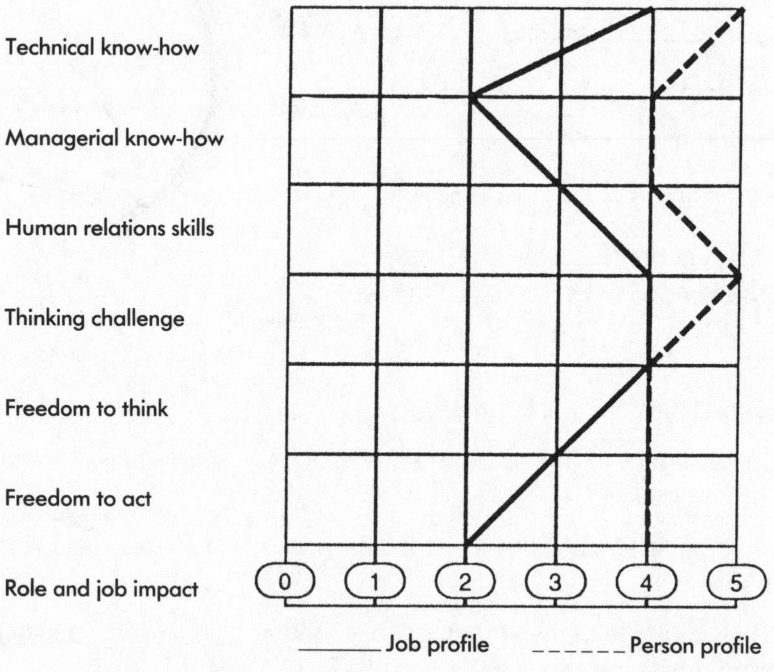

Figure 4.2 Job requirement profile versus person profile

Step 5: Documentation of results

The documented output from the panel discussions consisted of:

- a potential list giving a detailed survey of managers with the greatest potential as well as showing the gaps between job requirements and individual potential;
- detailed information about the potential of each manager against a range of jobs;
- information concerning career and succession planning;
- information regarding appropriate development that should take place across the organisation;
- the particular strengths and development needs for each manager to form the basis of individual development plans/action.

Figure 4.3 shows an example of a potential inventory.

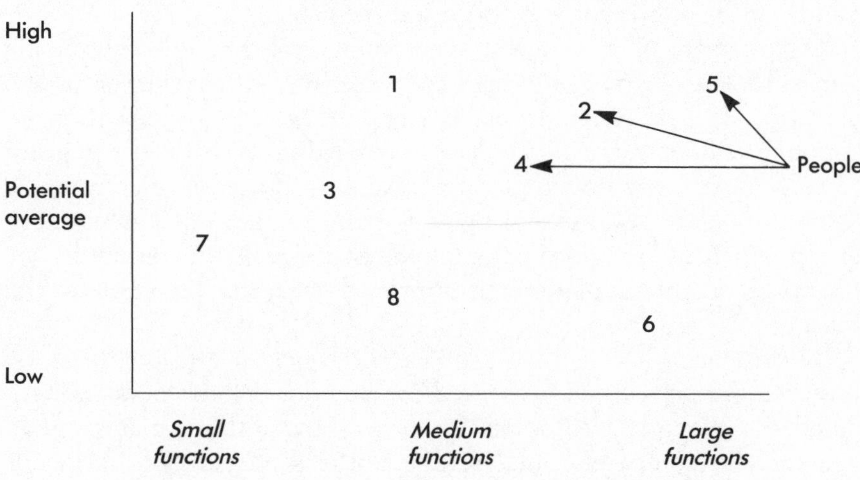

Figure 4.3 Results of potential appraisal: department manager

Step 6: Action plan

The results of the potential assessment provided useful information for use in succession planning. The data made it possible to determine whether new recruits were needed for certain jobs and what the current requirement profiles for managerial jobs in this organisation were. The company was able to determine which individuals had the current potential to move into different jobs and which person suited each requirement profile.

HOW IT WORKED IN PRACTICE

To begin with the profile of the job to be filled was described in terms of a job requirement profile (as described in Steps 1 and 2). The job profile could be evaluated by weighted summation of required job criteria levels. All managers with approximately the same profile were then selected. Once the managers, with adequate potential for the job, had been selected it was important to check they had the relevant background and experience, ie that they met the technical know-how and situation specific criteria. For example, if a research and development divisional manager position was to be filled, managers with an R and D background would be on the short list.

The manager who showed the potential level demanded by the job and had relevant practical experience took first place in the succession plan (this has been developed in Chapter 2). This organisation, in common with many large organisations, used a succession organigram to assist it with succession planning. An example of an organigram is shown in Figure 4.4. Further benefits from the potential assessment exercise included the production of personal development profiles for the management population and improved salary management for the business.

By comparing managerial profiles with current and potential job requirement profiles, personalised development plans could be instigated. For example, if interview analyses showed that a manager had a low level of competence in developing others, measures could be put in place to develop this managerial competency. Development activities could be tailored to the manager's current environment and

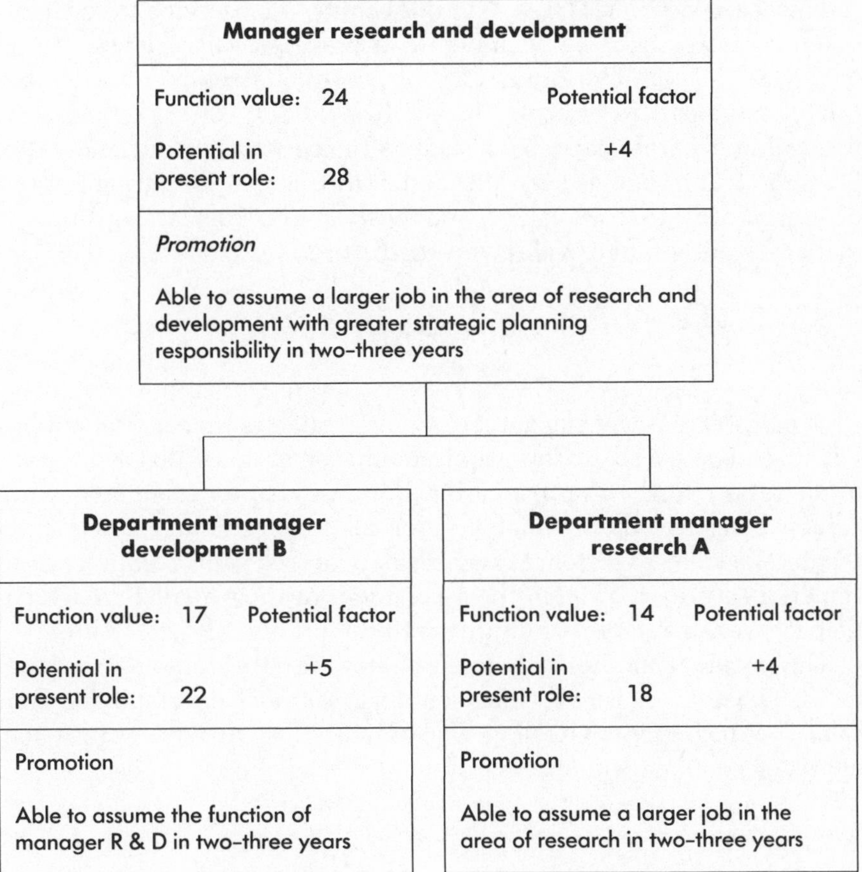

Figure 4.4 Succession planning organigram

preferred learning style. Activities could include adopting, as a mentor, a senior manager or peer particularly skilled in developing others. The manager could be given a special project involving work in this area, or invited to attend a training programme specifically focusing on this competency.

By collating managerial competency profiles, the organisation or particular divisions within the organisation could undertake a development needs analysis, so that specific types of personnel development could be planned and budgeted for.

The organisation referred to in this chapter also decided to consider potential assessment as an input to managerial salary level. Many organisations combine the results of potential assessment with the salary management process. In addition to the classic criteria for determining base salary, such as experience and performance, the potential factor can also be considered. In this way the organisation communicates that it values and wishes to retain the group of managers on whom it will rely in the future.

SUMMARY

This method of analysing future potential enables managerial potential to be compared to the requirements of various jobs within an organisation. In the example outlined in this chapter managers were assessed against their suitability for all requirements of a job ie technical skills, experience and display of relevant competencies. Superiors were involved in the assessment of their managers, which helped to ensure their commitment to the process and its results.

The results from the assessment of managerial potential were used in many ways, eg succession planning, personal development and salary management, enabling the organisation to take a strategic approach to management development.

5

Performance Management – Where Is It Going?

Frank Hartle
Hay Group, UK

In a recent survey in the UK over 80 per cent of the 1,750 organisations surveyed had some kind of performance management arrangements[1]. Surveys in other parts of Western Europe have revealed similar ratios. It is now widely recognised as an important management process. But in the same survey the majority of personnel managers said that their performance management arrangements were only partly effective or ineffective. In this chapter we will answer four questions:

- What is performance management?
- In what circumstances is it likely to be most effective?
- How is performance management developing?
- What is total performance management?

PERFORMANCE MANAGEMENT: A DEFINITION

Performance management is a term that is widely used today, but there is no commonly agreed definition. In some organisations it is regarded as another name for management by objectives. In others it is something to do only with the appraisal of individuals. Others have parcelled it into an annual event associated with training and development, or a process relating to performance related pay. These are relatively narrow definitions of performance management. We believe that it is a holistic process which can embrace all these elements – and some more. A frequently used description is:

> a process or set of processes for establishing shared understanding about what is to be achieved (and how it is to be achieved), and of managing people in a way that increases the probability that it will be achieved.

Within this definition organisations can take a broad view of how the performance management process encompasses the way people are managed and what elements are included in it. The process could embrace:

- strategy and objectives;
- job definition;
- objective setting;
- coaching and counselling;
- performance review;
- skills training;
- performance related pay;
- training and development.

We believe that the performance management process is more likely to be successful if it is operated as a single integrated process, rather than a set of separate and sometimes unrelated processes (see Figure 5.1). We see the performance management process as an integrated cycle of performance planning (definition of job responsibilities, setting performance expectations, goal or objective setting at the beginning of the period); performance coaching (monitoring, feedback coaching, development); and performance review (formal performance appraisal at the end of the period) conducted between managers and employees to

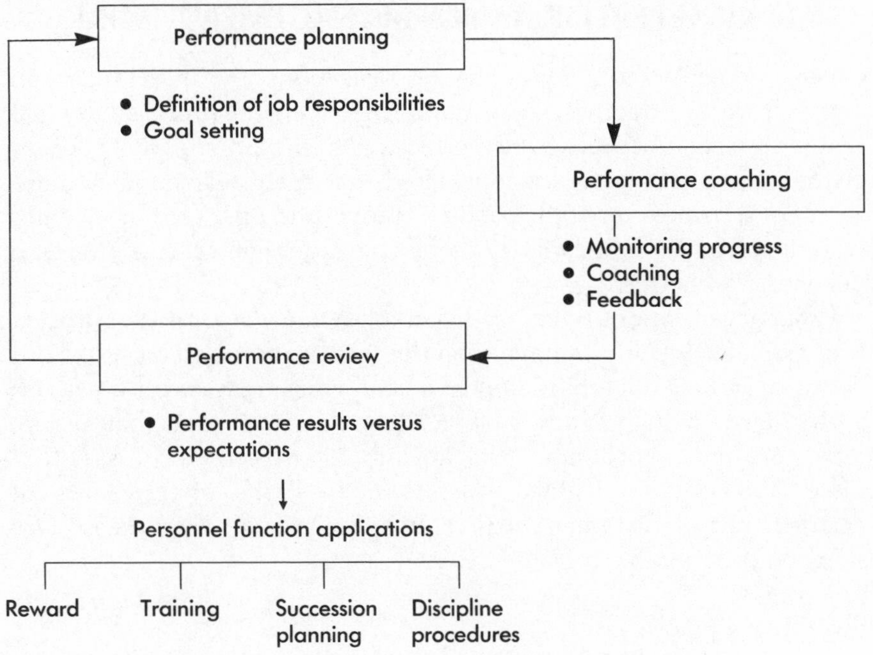

Figure 5.1 The performance management process – an integrated cycle

track and improve individual and corporate performance and to provide information for one or more personnel functions.

As an integrated process it ensures that employees:

- are aware of what is expected of them and how their contribution fits into the 'big picture';
- have been involved in establishing the objectives they are required to achieve;
- receive appropriate support and coaching throughout the period;
- understanding how their performance is to be measured and can track how well they are doing;
- are given challenges that they feel are important but attainable;
- are given appropriate recognition and reward for their achievements.

MAKING PERFORMANCE MANAGEMENT WORK

Given the potential benefits that organisations and individuals can derive from an effective performance management process why is it that many schemes seem to be ineffective? In the UK study 68 per cent of the personnel managers considered that their performance management schemes were only partly effective, and 7 per cent of schemes were ineffective. This is likely to be the experience across Western Europe. Why is this?

What organisations have learned in the last few years is that process is the key. In the UK we have seen the results of research carried out at one of our clients where we have been working for over a year on performance management. The research clearly showed that, where managers and subordinates had carefully followed the processes that were laid out and trained, their rating of the effectiveness of performance management was higher than where the process was skimped or ignored.

Setting up a process

The first step is to clarify why you want the process. What do you want it to achieve for you? Various studies of those organisations with formal performance management arrangements have revealed a number of reasons for introducing the process, eg in the IPM study:

Table 5.1 Reasons for introducing performance management

Purpose	Percentage of organisations
Improve organisational effectiveness	85
Motivate employees	57
Improve training and development	54
Change culture	54
Link pay to productivity	50
Attract and retain specialists	45
Support total quality management	36
Link pay to skills development	16
Manage wage bill	14

Source: IPM

Many organisations fail to focus on just one or two clear outcomes. They have unrealistic expectations of what the process can deliver. The business works best when a few critical outcomes are aimed at.

The second step is to design the process that fits the purposes. It is likely that the process varies within the organisation to reflect different functions and jobs. Some jobs are more easily measured through their outputs; other jobs are measured through acquisition or demonstration of behaviours or competencies; others will be a combination of outputs and competencies. All jobs can be defined in terms of 'what success looks like', whether it is outputs, behaviours, skills or a combination of these. Performance management applies to all jobs and not just 'operational type' jobs.

The third step is to provide thorough training for all staff involved in the process. There are two objectives for the training phase – first, to develop the appropriate skills involved in the performance management process, eg objective-setting, coaching and appraising. Second, to develop a sense of ownership and commitment in line managers, to the process. It is critically important that line managers play an active role in the training programme. They are key to the performance management process – they deliver it to their staff and it is only through their skills and commitment that the process will become effective. Strong engagement from senior managers is vital – these influential people should drive and steer the programme and they should demonstrate a commitment to the process through their own behaviours.

It is important that the training programme is stretched over a full performance cycle. This enables skills to be developed at the appropriate stage in the cycle. Also it keeps up the momentum of the process by providing advice and support to the line managers and staff over a 12-month period (as a minimum).

The fourth step is to audit continually the impact of the process. Is it fulfilling its purposes? Can it be improved next year? Does it fit all situations and jobs? Does it need to be modified? Performance management is a learning process: it will not be absolutely right in the first year or two, but with careful review and appropriate revisions it will get better and better.

Taking these four steps increases the probability of success in introducing a performance management process into your organisation.

However, what can you do if you have a performance management process already in place which is not very effective? First you should identify where it is not adding value. This means carrying out an audit of the process through a survey of appraisers and apraisees to identify the critical performance issues. Then you need to plan a strategy for improvement. Some organisations might decide to go for 'small wins' – tackling one issue at a time, setting realistic goals for success, taking actions and assessing results. The small wins approach is relatively cautious and is likely to take a long time before there is a step change in performance throughout the organisation. But it is based on a sound philosophy – small wins are realistically attainable; and lead to bigger wins in the long term.

But other organisations might want to go for a complete re-think of their existing process and look for quicker ways of increasing their effectiveness. Like many other aspects of managing people, the search for improvements seems endless. New forms of performance management are emerging.

DEVELOPMENTS IN PERFORMANCE MANAGEMENT

A closer link with business strategy

Organisations are making increasing, explicit use of performance management processes to communicate and reinforce overall strategy and culture, such as a focus on quality improvements or customer service. The performance management process accomplishes these objectives by ensuring that employees' accountabilities and objectives relate directly to organisational strategy and objectives. The organisation's plans are cascaded down the organisation, through line managers.

A continuous integrated process

Another key development is the broadening of performance management beyond the annual objective setting and appraisal interview. There is widespread dissatisfaction with the 'annual event'. Organisations are increasingly paying more attention to the other 364 days of the year when management of performance is part of day-to-day boss/ subordinate relationships.

The development of skills and competencies

There has been a tendency for performance management schemes in the past to neglect the developmental aspects ie identifying individual developmental needs and planning how these needs can be filled. The concept of separate appraisals – one for development purposes and one for achievement review, is gaining ground, as is the idea that annual reviews are often, in any case, too infrequent really to assist in improving performance. The development of skills and competencies can be facilitated by the use of behaviourally-anchored scales that enable individuals to assess how much of the required skill/competency/behaviour they have been demonstrating.

Figure 5.2 shows a behaviourally-anchored scale of communication that is used by a client organisation. It has three sets of behaviour descriptions that are used to enable judgements on five levels of performance. To improve performance, the manager, as coach, together with the job holder, must determine the skills or competencies requiring further development and describe how these improvements will be achieved. These behaviour descriptions enable individual job holders to imagine a picture of what better performance looks like.

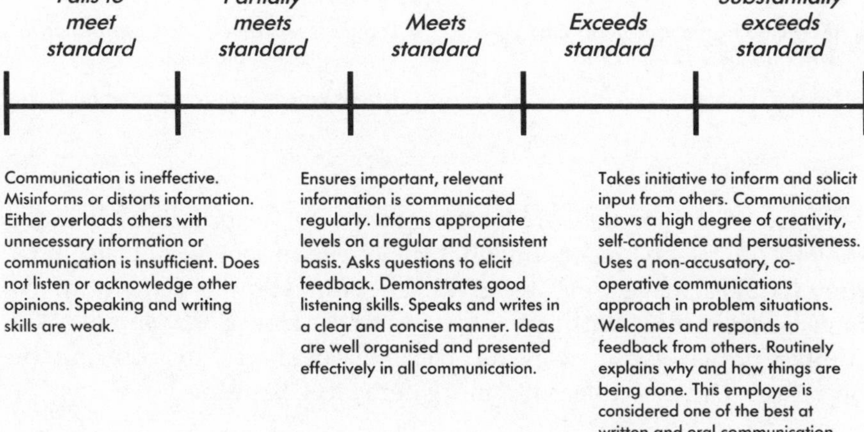

Figure 5.2 Scale of communication

Mixed models of performance management

The dominant trend in performance management systems has been to pay for performance, despite a widely-held feeling that such schemes are difficult to implement and rarely succeed in meeting their objective. Recently there has been a movement against pure pay-for-performance systems as a result of doubts about their effectiveness and their applicability to the rapidly changing, team oriented business environment of the future. What is emerging is a mixed model process that focuses on competencies (the underlying characteristics of an individual that predict effective or superior performance in a job). Organisations that are oriented to the future are moving to balance pay-for-performance with pay-for-competencies. Table 5.2 summarises how pay-for-performance and pay-for-competencies differ on certain key variables.

Table 5.2 Mixed models

In mixed models performance and competencies are considered	
(50–90 per cent)	(10–50 per cent)
Performance (Pay-for-results)	Competencies (Pay-for-skills)
• The 'what' of performance	• The 'how' of performance
• Quantitative	• More qualitative
• Short time frame: one year, past performance in present job	• Longer time frame: future performance in present and future job
• Reward oriented	• Development (behaviour change) oriented

These mixed models are potentially powerful processes because they focus the job holders on what they have to achieve and also how they should achieve their objectives. The competencies defined should have a direct link with the objectives set. Hence development of competency levels increases the probability of success in achieving the objectives. (This is covered in more detail in Chapter 6.)

TOTAL PERFORMANCE MANAGEMENT

Increasingly, as organisations gain experience with performance management, it is being recognised as a process that encapsulates both the aims of the organisation to improve its performance and the aims of the individuals to improve theirs. Putting the two together in the context of the employment relationship is at the heart of total performance management. This is an all-embracing process – a holistic approach – that acts as a vehicle for strategy implementation and culture change. At the individual level it is characterised by the mixed model plan, combining the what and how of performance, ie business/job objectives and behavioural/developmental objectives (see Figure 5.3).

The main issue with the formulation of any vision or mission statement is making it happen, ie translating it into action. Some organisations have recognised that the performance management process provides a suitable vehicle for communicating the mission statement, converting it into realistic and achievable objectives, monitoring progress and assessing achievements. The personal

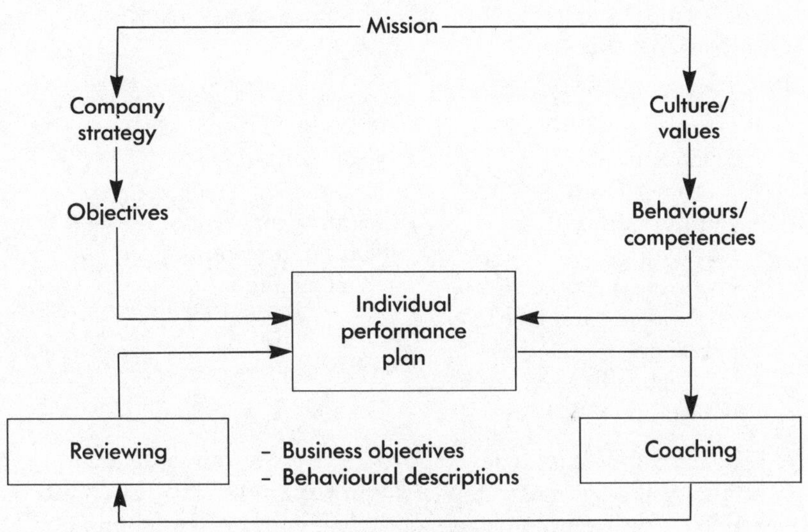

Figure 5.3 Total performance management

objectives that are set embrace the business and the behavioural objectives that emanate from the company's objectives.

Two case studies illustrate how the total performance management process is being developed in two different organisations.

Case 1: Total performance management in a major chemical company

The company's goal was to strive continually for improved performance at all levels. Their 'performance excellence' process was designed to encourage open, on-going communication between the manager and the employee about performance issues. The highlights of the process are:

- focused performance objectives (linked to company objectives);
- personal/professional development objectives;
- professional and managerial competencies;
- employee involvement, continuous feedback and discussion of performance throughout the year.

The company defined the set of competencies expected for professional success as:

Professional competencies

- planning and project management;
- customer focus;
- communication;
- teamwork;
- problem solving;
- professional and technical excellence;
- safety, health and environmental affairs.

Managerial competencies

- leadership;
- delegation;
- managing change;
- performance management;
- human resources management.

For each competency it developed a set of behaviourally-anchored rating scales (as illustrated in Figure 5.2). This focused each employee on a set of business objectives and the development of key competencies. This is their performance contract.

This particular company uses the performance management process to demonstrate its commitment to quality service and customer focus. Figure 5.4 shows how the competencies in customer focus were defined in terms of specific behaviours:

- Contributes to the company's commitment to provide the highest quality products and service to internal and external customers.
- Initiates actions to identify and meet internal and external customer expectations.
- Acts in a manner that makes it easy for customers to do business with you.
- Creates a positive image of the company with all external customers.

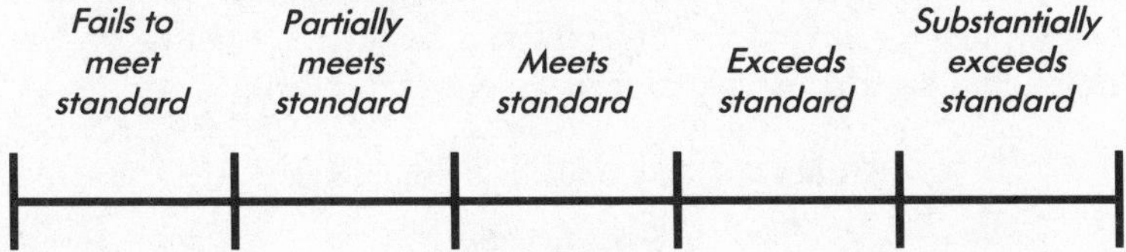

Not genuinely committed to equality ideals and principles of customer focus. Does not try to understand our customers' expectations or improve the delivery of services. Is often unwilling to change priorities to meet customers' expectations.

Strives to understand and meet the expectations of internal and external customers. Is service-oriented: responsive to requests from others, available and approachable on a routine basis and in emergencies. Initiates actions to improve the process and the quality of products or services delivered. Meets frequently with customers and solicits feedback.

Is a role model of the Company's principle of customer focus. Places high priority on the development on internal and external customer relationships. Gathers the necessary resources from all departments and individuals to ensure outstanding delivery of service to customers. Encourages others to take initiative to provide continuous improvement concepts to the delivery of products and services.

Figure 5.4 Competencies in relation to customer focus

Case 2: Total performance management in a manufacturing company

In this example the company set out to improve its business performance in a highly competitive environment by sharpening up its business planning procedures, by ensuring greater individual accountability for action and results and by focusing all employees on six key values.

- commitment to a safe and healthy environment;
- commitment to customer satisfaction;
- respect for individuals;
- promotion of teamwork;
- commitment to continuous improvement;
- recognition and reward for achievement.

Each value has been translated into behavioural descriptions (as in the previous case study) and this provides a framework for individuals to determine a personal development plan alongside a set of key performance objectives. The key elements of the individual performance plan are shown in Table 5.3.

Table 5.3 Individual performance plan

Key objectives

Name:	**Job Title:**	**Department:**	
Key objectives	*Measurement of performance*	*Agreed performance standards*	*Indicate if priority (P)*
1. Improve safety at work standards	• Accident statistics • Compliance with company standards	• Reduce by 5 per cent all reported accidents • 100 per cent compliance by end 1992	(P) (P)
2. Implementation of performance management process	• Timeliness • Audit of staff involved	• Implemented to first level managers by end Q3 • 65 per cent first-level managers give favourable comments on process	
3. Complete restructuring of department	• Redeployment of staff • New job descriptions issued	• Completed by end Q2 • Completed by end Q3	(P) (P)
4. Production capability	• Production targets • Costs per unit	• Produce 450 kilotons/year • Stay within production budget	(P) (P)

Using this total performance management approach the company hopes to achieve long-term and sustained improved business performance and organisational effectiveness.

The link to a total quality initiative

Some organisations might wish to focus the performance management process on one major organisational goal, eg a commitment to quality service. Many organisations are going down the quality route. The value of linking the quality initiative to the performance management process is that it increases the probability that quality initiatives will be achieved. The performance management process – of planning, coaching, reviewing and rewarding – should ensure that the quality goals are clarified, focused on, acted on, given support and feedback and ultimately recognised if they are achieved.

Until a few years ago quality was 'added on' in a fragmented way. Now it is widely recognised that a quality initiative requires:

- a total corporate approach;
- integration into the whole business;
- a major culture change.

These are the elements of a focused total performance process, with the 'lens' being a customer care programme. The linking of a total quality initiative to the performance management process is set out in Figure 5.5.

SUMMARY

Performance management exists in many forms in most organisations. In some organisations it exists as a low-impact process concerned with objective-setting and/or the annual appraisal. Other organisations, particularly those looking to the future and those concerned with improving business performance by focusing on behavioural aspects of performance, see the performance management process as the vehicle for making it happen – a powerful high

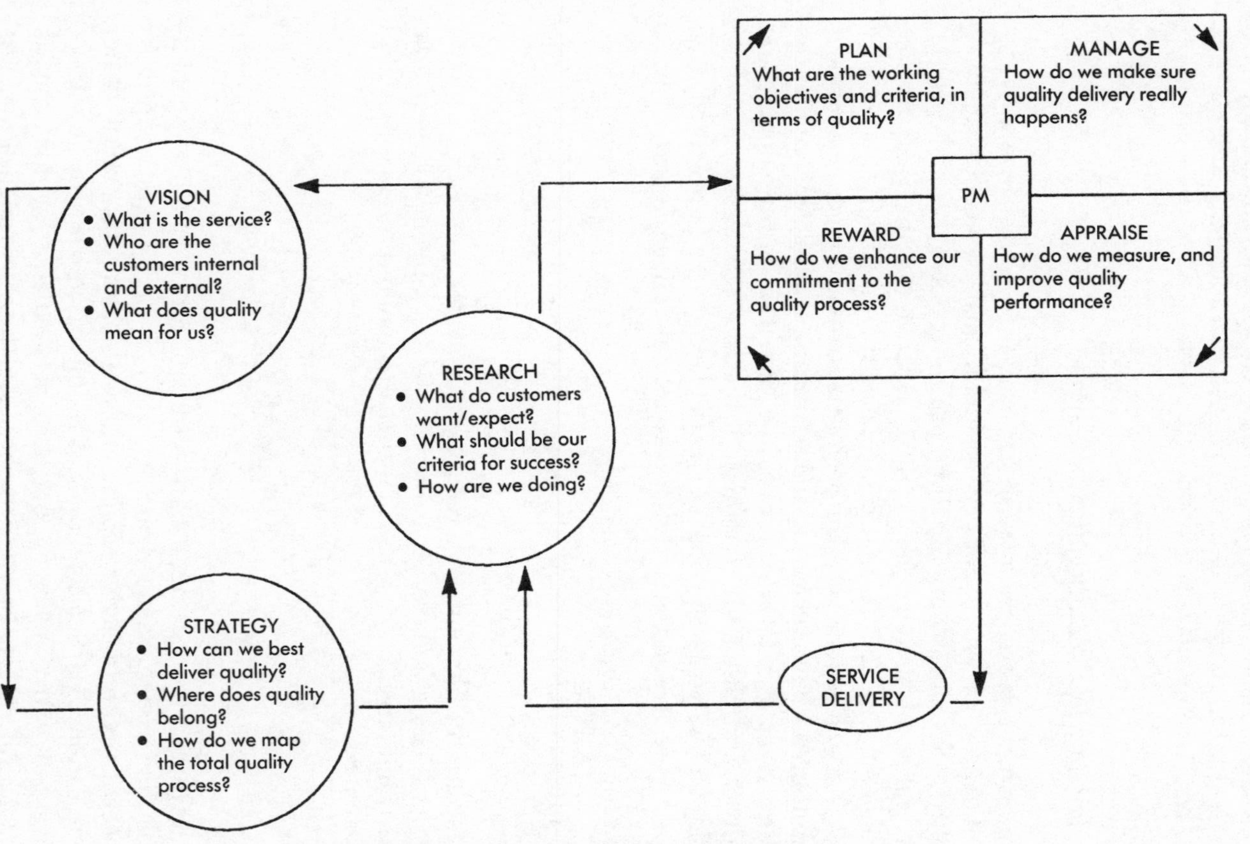

Figure 5.5 Linking total quality and performance management

value-added process. We know that performance management is difficult and costly in terms of time. It cannot be introduced or changed overnight. It has to be assembled bit by bit, often over many years, with each part in need of regular review, maintenance and improvement. But it is the glue that holds together and integrates all human resource initiatives. And we know that it does work in many organisations. So recognise it as a long journey: once started it is difficult to stop but not starting at all is not an option either.

REFERENCE

1. Long, P (1986) *Performance Appraisal Revisited* Institute of Personnel Management.

6

Paying for Competency – What Does It Mean?

David Fitt
Hay Group, UK

> 'As soon as you begin paying for "nice to have" characteristics divorced from job accountabilities which measure value added to the firm, you lose control of your compensation system.'

> 'Competency in many jobs *is* performance; unless we base our policies and pay systems on people's capabilities, our business simply won't succeed.'

This chapter will address a range of issues on the broad spectrum between these contrasting views and propose a framework for recognising competency through pay that is tenable, consistent and practical.

PAYMENT FOR WHAT?

There has never been greater interest in the idea of paying people for their skills and competencies rather than the job that they occupy. It has become an increasingly popular topic at seminars and conferences; it is stimulating an increasing number of articles in the professional journals[1]; and it is certainly a live issue in terms of the number of enquiries to this consultancy from organisations that are clearly enthusiastic about the concept but are unsure how to move forward.

What seems to be missing in the debate so far is a clear definition of what 'paying for competency' actually means; what pay systems that incorporate the principle look like; and, most importantly, what the implications are of moving in the direction of competency-based pay for job evaluation schemes, performance appraisal schemes and salary administration policies and systems.

The business issues that have placed this area centre stage on many human resource directors' agendas have been extensively described in Chapter 1. They include:

- the trend towards 'flatter', de-layered organisations that inspire and depend on individual initiative and capability rather than detailed job definition;
- the role of competencies in enabling and driving organisational change;
- the increasing importance of 'knowledge workers' in securing the current and future success of organisations.

They also include matters relating to pay:

- the association of job evaluation schemes with bureaucracy, wasted management time and 'control' from the centre;
- the growing dissatisfaction with traditional job evaluation-based salary structures and salary ranges in terms of their ability to reflect and reward performance;
- the developing interest in competencies as increasingly well validated dimensions of performance and career development.

Factors affecting pay

From these issues emerges the case for recognising people's capabilities and qualities more fundamentally in pay systems. The question is, how? This requires a consideration of the factors that affect the way people in organisations are paid. A model that describes the main

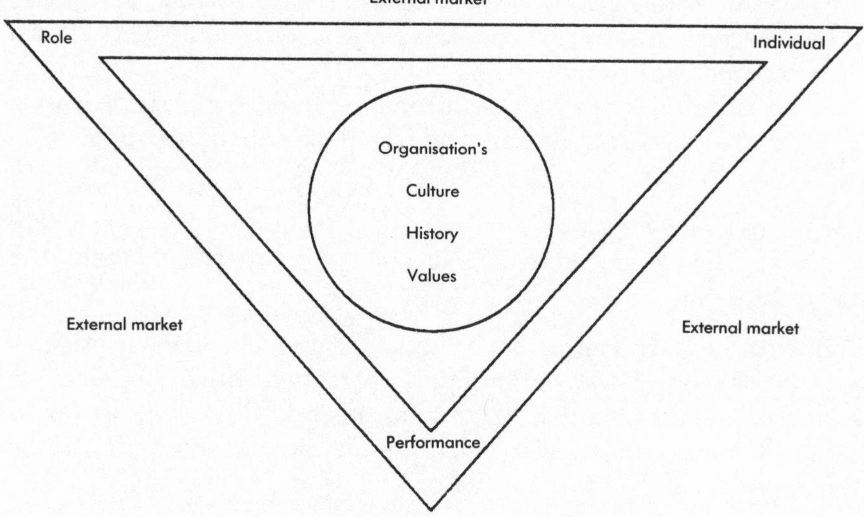

Figure 6.1 Compensable factors affecting payment

variables simply but comprehensively is shown in Figure 6.1. The core is the triangle and its three points.

Role relates to the nature of the job/role/responsibilities being performed by an individual. It may be a permanent, well defined role, or can be extremely variable, consisting of project-type roles that regularly change. At any time, however, this role and all the other roles in the organisation represent the way in which the organisation's mission and strategy are being discharged. As such, it has a value, both in terms of internal relativities and, as we shall see, the external market.

Individual describes the competencies possessed by an individual in the organisation. Competencies (as we have seen in the preceding chapters) include every kind of skill, area of knowledge, trait, motive, characteristic. Here I must define my terms very specifically. 'Competency' in fact has two kinds of meaning:

1. Areas of *competence* or skills and knowledge that can be acquired through study, experience, practice; they include functional (often vocational and professional) knowledge, and a large

number of generic work activities (eg setting objectives, planning, making presentations), as typically defined in national competence frameworks.

2. *Competencies* that are the deeper seated traits and personal qualities possessed by individuals, which are harder to develop and change.

For the rest of the chapter I will use these terms in this sense; where I intend the more general indication of capability I will use 'competence'.

Performance is the expression of how well an individual has played a part in delivering the organisation's strategy, either in terms of achieving specific objectives relating to the individual's role, and/or in demonstrating competences that are defined as relevant to the organisation – either in a particular role, or more generally.

Internal and external factors
These three principal dimensions interact within two environments, internal and external.

The **culture** of the organisation represents an accumulated set of attitudes and values that are both inherited and reflective of the organisation's current direction. Relevant examples would be the importance of 'fairness' in pay decisions, or the extent to which performance-related elements should form a major part of total pay.

External influences include, for example, the market value of particular skills/competences possessed by individuals, or of jobs defined in a common way by an industry; the way in which other organisations pay their people and create a norm at any time.

WHICH FACTORS ARE CRITICAL?

All pay decisions reflect these elements, consciously or unconsciously. Our task is to assess the relationship between them, with particular reference to the extent to which individual competences can be rewarded.

In practical terms, the debate about job and job evaluation driven pay systems stems from the fact that relative job size has become the traditional starting point from which pay structures are built: in other words, *role* is the independent variable in our model. It is difficult to imagine a pay system for a significant number of employees in an organisation that does not require *one* of the three dimensions of the triangle to have this function. So we need to look at whether the other two elements can be so considered.

Performance cannot really be considered a candidate outside a very narrow set of circumstances. For example, people being paid exclusively on a piece-work or commission basis might be considered to fall into this category; but it is inappropriate as a basis for paying all employees in the great majority of organisations. Performance, as we will see, is really the main dependent variable in pay terms, representing the extent to which role-defined objectives have been delivered, or required behaviours displayed. Defined in this way, it is of fundamental importance to our subject in this chapter because, in the form of competency-based appraisal or performance management, we will find a major vehicle for rewarding competencies. But it is not a potential starting point for us.

So we come to the other main alternative: can the *individual* dimension be considered as the starting point for pay systems that wish to recognise competences? This implies some form of 'sizing' system that values individuals differentially according to their capabilities. Many examples of such systems appear to be available: multi-skilling frameworks, which offer increased base salary as additional skills and qualifications are gained; 'skills matrices', which describe areas of capability in a particular organisation and construct grade or pay relativities according to an individual's mix of skills; and, more recently and more radically, frameworks using only deeper-seated competencies, usually for members of a particular job family (eg research scientists). These all look like the real thing: 'pure' capability driving the core differentials on which other elements of the pay structure are based.

But a little reflection quickly shows that this conclusion is superficial. In order to construct these frameworks, it has been necessary to ask the question, 'capability for what?' In most cases, the 'what' is the value to the organisation of different roles delivering results or contribution. Hence, the multi-skilled framework is based on the value of a multi-skilled worker, calibrated to take account of the value of subsets of these skills; the skills matrix and the professional career structure are based on a relatively conventional view of the relative value of common roles performed by people in the structure. This is not to gainsay the value of expressing the frameworks in this way: they send powerful messages to individuals that increasing competence is desired by the organisation and the means of career progression for the individual. But the framework itself derives from a concept of role size.

How job evaluation has developed

This brings us back to the third dimension in our model – role – and the traditional starting point for pay systems to which we had been trying to find an alternative. This does not mean that the competence-based frameworks are untenable. What it means is that we need to understand better what role-based approaches actually consist of.

The history of analytical job evaluation methods is an interesting one. As early as the 1930s, examples of both points factor and factor comparison schemes were widespread in progressive organisations, and observers and practitioners had already noted that there were, in fact, only three basic kinds of factors: skills; effort; and responsibility. Each of these could be expressed by a greater number of sub-factors, but (with the exception of working conditions, which for the purpose of this discussion I will exclude as a factor) all schemes addressed the same questions: What is the level of responsibility of this job within the organisation? What is the nature of the skills required to carry that responsibility? How intensively do they need to be applied?

Points rating and factor comparison schemes proceed in somewhat different directions. Points schemes use as many factors as are necessary to describe the range of jobs under consideration; comparison schemes, comparing as they do the proportional score in each factor, restrict the number of factors so their definition becomes generalised. But in both cases the factors on which the ultimate 'size' of the total number depends, are overwhelmingly the factors relating to skill and effort. Thus, the relative proportion of the points for a job with little organisational responsibility will typically be 90 per cent skill and effort, 10 per cent responsibility; that for a senior professional specialist 75 per cent skill and effort; and, in our experience[2], those for senior executives in the largest organisations in excess of 60 per cent for skill and effort. In other words, most of the judgements, and by far the greatest proportion of the total, relate to the kind of factors that we have just been considering in competence-based sizing schemes. All that is different is that, in traditional job or role evaluation approaches, the correlation between the organisational requirement of a role (responsibility) and the individual capability required to carry it out are made explicit in the method.

It is artificially simplistic to attempt to separate the 'role' and 'individual' dimensions when seeking options for the basis of a consistent pay system. Apparent competence-driven schemes are in fact dependent on an underlying assumption of role requirement; and all analytical job evaluation schemes consist principally of areas of competence closely correlated with role requirement.

This understanding takes us a long way towards an appreciation of some of the fundamental underlying principles in pay system design and also places in context some of the comments about job evaluation that have enjoyed recent popularity. While there may be some basis for the criticisms that have been levelled at job evaluation's associated bureaucracy, procedures and control mechanisms, no real alternative is available to its concept of role importance as the independent variable in pay systems in the great majority of organisations.

HOW COMPETENCY DRIVES PAY

So how does this understanding help our consideration of competences as fundamental drivers of pay? There are four main categories:

1. *Competences as sizing factors.* The use of competences as the skill and effort factors in schemes where more abstract factors had been used in the past.
2. *Investing in competence.* Recognising the level of current individual competence, or providing an incentive for individuals to acquire additional competencies to improve the future capability of the organisation.
3. *Wider pay bands.* Less precision in the way in which fine differences in 'size' are translated into pay/grade structures.
4. *Competency-based performance management.* Wider definitions of competency can be used explicitly as the main variables on which individuals' progression through a pay band is based.

Competences as sizing factors

Having established the fundamental relationship between the 'input' factors in a scheme and the role requirement, a number of options are available for describing them more specifically so that they relate to the organisation's own context. This is where skill matrices and job family models can provide a description of the capabilities needed to be successful in a particular organisation. For a defined population, generic areas of capability are defined in an interactive process with managers and employees that best describes the variables in that population. Figure 6.2 shows the factors that were developed for a professional engineering structure; note in particular the varieties of 'know-how' that are given more subtle expression in this framework. A more generic framework can be developed for managers at a particular level in an organisation. Scales showing different levels of each factor are developed as part of the definition process.

Where the nature of roles in the population is relatively static, key roles are described using the appropriate level of each skill; in a more

Engineering job family

Factors
Knowledge
Application of knowledge
Integration
Autonomy
People management
Management of relationships
Creativity
Project management

Factor definition
Integration 'Your ability to integrate directly technologies, skills or knowledge'

Factor levels
1. Capable of working within own speciality
2. Capable of co-ordinating some elements within a speciality
3. Capable of integrating all elements within a speciality
4. Capable of integrating a group of specialities within a discipline, or a number of relevant disciplines on a project, component, process or system
5. Capable of the integration of all specialities within a discipline, or the integration of all relevant disciplines on a major project, component, process or system

Figure 6.2 Example of skill matrix factor and definitions

flexible organisation where an infinite variety of roles may appear, a points rating scheme is developed to 'size' each role. These schemes are powerful in describing what skills are needed in the job. They work best when used for relatively narrowly defined populations (eg engineers, analysts/programmers, a sales career hierarchy). For larger, more diverse populations in large organisations, a number of different frameworks may be needed, related to each other by a common sizing system using more abstract skill factors.

However, the types of capability described here are essentially areas of competence, using the definition established earlier. They share elements of role and person, in that they can usually be expressed equally well in terms of 'required to' (role) or 'capable of' (person). But they are not true competencies in the sense of deep-seated qualities.

In our consulting work with clients, we have yet to find skill-based factors in a matrix of this kind (used to drive a core pay structure) that include true competencies of the deep-seated kind. The closest approach is in broadly defined professional families where some competencies, expressed at different levels of intensity, correlate closely with size and differentiate levels. An example would be competencies developed for research scientists. But outside such structures, it is difficult either to generalise about levels of competency, or to find the behavioural indicators (critical for the successful operation of any competency assessment process) which apply universally. Competencies are fundamentally indicators of performance or potential that (in terms of our definition) are dependent variables. Indeed, they relate to areas of competence and can be correlated with them to show how they enable people to be competent in those areas. But they cannot be used as skill factors for sizing and pay structure design purposes.

Investing in competence

It has generally been in inviolable principle of all grading/sizing systems that an individual needs to be graded and paid on the basis of the role actually being performed. In situations where an individual's capabilities exceed the requirements of a particular role, or the requirements of a standard recruitment level, it should, however, be possible to pay/grade them at a higher level as long as an economic case can be made for such a premium. Methodology based on clear cost-benefit analysis typically describes the individual in this situation as an asset in which additional funds are invested in the probability of a future economic return, over and above that which would normally be expected from someone in the role. A simple example would be a salesperson identified as having competencies substantially better than baseline requirements who, recruited at a premium, outperforms colleagues and realises the investment in a two-year period.

This is paying for competency in the form of *potential* to deliver in the future. As such it is a genuine form of pay related to deep-seated competencies as it is these personal qualities that will usually differentiate outstanding from average performers. The economic evaluation needs to be carried out rigorously if the procedure is to be defensible and equitable in a large organisation. But it is justifiable and, arguably, highly desirable.

The principle also applies to 'areas of competence'; it occurs most frequently through multi-skilling frameworks designed to increase people's skills or know-how in a defined area. In a sense, an 'ultimate' totally multi-skilled role is defined for a group of people, and they are given the incentive to work towards acquiring as many of them as possible. The economic argument here is clear – it is competence for a defined purpose. An example is shown in Figure 6.3.

The more radical version of this involves taking some risks in specifying the future competences, because the nature of work in a fast-moving industry is not yet clear. One example would be an employer who specifies that a minimum proportion of all new graduates must have a substantial expertise in IT principles and

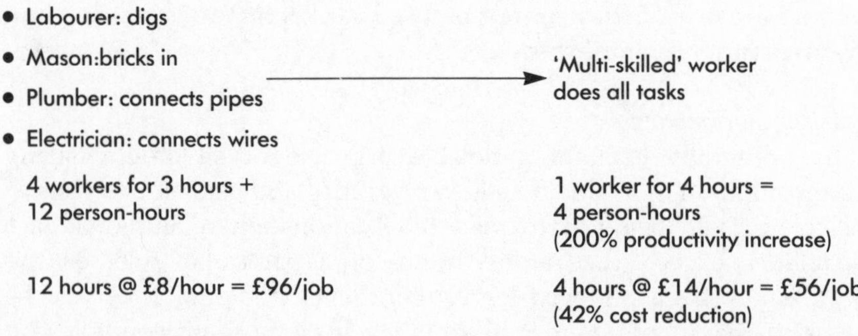

Figure 6.3 Cost-benefit justification of pay for 'multi-skilling' – Installing water meters

applications; another more familiar example is providing an incentive to current employees to acquire a business qualification on a part-time basis. The important distinction is that the precise nature of any future role is not yet clear: higher levels of knowledge and competence will not bring a short-term advantage, but are judged to provide a basis for future success.

Criteria for appointment or promotion in these cases are not always as rigorous as they might be. If no economic evaluation is carried out, a management control process is necessary to ensure that individuals are being matched to the level of accountability for which they are being paid. Failure to do this leads to a kind of 'competency drift' that is potentially more damaging and expensive than conventional grade drift.

Wider pay bands

The attention paid to the development of competencies in recent years, the research findings that demonstrate that an improvement in performance of one standard deviation in a job is worth on average 80 per cent of salary[3], and the growth in performance-related pay schemes all bring us to the single most important element in paying for competency: variable pay based on required competencies demonstrated on the job. This will be covered in more detail in the next section. First it is worth considering the way in which many organisations have recognised the fact that the independent variable – role – drives most basic pay structures, and yet has minimised its effect.

This has been through the adoption of grade structures with particularly wide bands, typically encompassing as many as three or four old 'just noticeably different' grades of a former structure. This approach generalises the level of contribution required of individuals, reduces the time spent on job evaluation and provides much greater scope for both areas of competence and competencies to be recognised in pay. There are substantial risks in adopting this approach: rigorous assessment frameworks and control processes are required, and managers have to be trusted! However, as part of an overall programme of recognising performance by changing the balance between the three major variables in pay, it has much to commend it.

An example is the pay structure introduced by a major UK general insurance company in 1988. A core job evaluation process allocates jobs to broad grades. Within these grades line managers have discretion to progress individuals on the bass of demonstrated competence and performance. Competence frameworks are well defined and assessments are regularly made; managers make all decisions subject only to overall budget constraints. 'Role size' is still the core variable in differentiating levels: but its impact relative to the variables of performance and competence is considerably reduced. Other examples of wider grade bands are increasingly evident; in many cases progression is linked specifically to acquisition of areas of competence as well as offering discretionary increases.

Competency-based performance management

The way in which performance in a role is measured gives the most scope for recognising competency in any pay system. Referring back to the triangle model, it can be seen that performance is essentially of two types: the extent to which role-based requirements are delivered ('objectives': the core of most managerial performance management schemes); and the extent to which those competencies that represent high performance in the job are demonstrated by the individual.

Objectives-based assessments: advantages and problems

Objectives are the most appropriate performance measures when individuals have a high level of influence over and personal responsibility for, outcomes for which they are accountable. Good examples would be sales representatives for life insurance, foreign exchange dealers, and chief executives of most companies. Compared with other individuals in the same organisation, their impact on the result area is prime, even though other external factors (eg the state of the economy, competitor activity) will also hae some effect. Performance objectives in these cases should be SMART: specific, measurable, attainable, realistic and time-specific. Objectives as performance measures are less appropriate, however, in other circumstances:

- when individuals have less control over the outcome of particular areas of work (ie they provide support services, or buying decisions are strongly influenced by factors such as price or advertising;
- when jobs or accountabilities change rapidly (eg when people carry out a number of activities at the same time in project teams).

- when long-term goals are of primary importance (eg research scientists);
- when performance is better defined in behavioural rather than output terms (particularly relevant in interpersonal contact and customer service roles, for example).

Competencies-based assessments
In these cases, competencies describe (by definition) what makes people successful in the role in question, and can thus be used with confidence in assessing performance. Good examples are check-out assistant roles in a retail store, and air cabin crew. In both cases performance objectives are hard to quantify (they occur most naturally as negative standards, eg restricting customer complaints to a certain level); the behavioural indicators that underlie competencies are ideal, however.

Some of the competencies identified as important for air cabin crew are shown below. Four different levels are defined using specific behavioural indicators; each individual is assessed several times over each six-month period by different supervisors who form part of the flight crew; the assessments are combined and an overall performance rating derived that is used to determine the appropriate level of base salary increase. In this case, rigour in assessment was provided both through a validation exercise that ensured that the competencies were indeed those that correlated with high performance, and through multi-rated assessment against the scaled levels of indicator.

Cabin crew competencies

- Personal impact
- Customer care
- Resilience
- Efficiency
- Customer management
- Teamwork
- Adaptability

Example – Customer care

A concern for providing prompt, courteous and attentive service to all customers plus the ability to understand and interpret their concerns and feelings. Confidence in their own abilities to provide that service.

A Does not recognise customer needs, does not regularly demonstrate courtesy and cheerfulness to them, makes little effort to be responsive. May demonstrate a lack of confidence or awkwardness.

B Is consistently courteous and cheerful to customers, interprets obvious manifestation of their needs and has confidence to assist and provide service to them.

C Is consistently polite and cheerful and makes a special effort to address customers' needs, can interpret non-verbal communication and diagnose customers' needs when not explicitly stated. Shows confidence in own ability in new non-routine situations, but is not overbearing or 'showy'.

D Is consistently courteous and cheerful to customers even when under pressure. Interprets non-verbal behaviour from subtle cues and has a track record of successfully 'reading people'. Has complete confidence in own ability with a 'can-do' attitude to challenging situations. Conveys enthusiasm about the job and the airline.

Mixed model

For most areas of work, a mixture of objectives and competencies are the most appropriate solution. 'Mixed models' of this kind – for salespeople, managers and for professionals – provide the opportunity to define both the 'what' as well as the 'how' and 'why' of performance. Figure 6.4 shows an abstract from the competency framework used to assess senior managers in a major chemical manufacturer's performance management system. The overall rating in this case is the average competency assessment combined with an overall 'performance against objectives' assessment.

There are, of course, major policy considerations to be made if competencies are to be used in this way. Issues of quality of

Senior manager competencies

Summary list
Analytical thinking
Pattern recognition
Strategic thinking
Persuasion
Use of influence strategies
Personal impact
Motivating

Appraisal How often does the person you are rating demonstrate the behaviour in an effective way, when opportunities are given:

4 Very frequently
3 In some situations
2 Not very often
1 Never

Use of influence strategies Definition: The ability to develop and use effective strategies to influence others. Strategies involve sequences of actions or alternatives that are calculated in advance and which incorporate aspects of two other competencies. Persuasiveness and concern with personal impact.

Selects and screens information for others	4	3	2	1
Uses subtle strategies to influence others	4	3	2	1
Uses experts or third parties to influence others	4	3	2	1
Makes others feel ownership of one's own proposal	4	3	2	1

Pattern recognition Definition: The ability to identify patterns or connections between situations that are not obviously related and to identify the key or underlying issues in complex situations.

Sees connections or patterns not obvious to others	4	3	2	1
Condenses large amounts of data to useful form	4	3	2	1
Uses clear analogies in speech and writing	4	3	2	1
Rapidly identifies key issues in a complex situation	4	3	2	1
Overall rating	**4**	**3**	**2**	**1**

Figure 6.4 Example of competency-based performance management

measurement, openness of the process, and relative importance of the competencies against each other and against objectives will always arise: but the most fundamental issue is of course whether to pay for competency at all. The judging versus coaching dilemma raised by Douglas McGregor 30 years ago is still highly topical, and many organisations still prefer to use competency-based approaches exclusively with a developmental focus, so that individuals can learn and grow away from alleged carrot-and-stick incentive devices. Others, however, take the legitimate view that recognising total performance openly in pay decisions is a wholly consistent message to send to employees. Indeed, the most appropriate question to organisations that have doubts about rating and paying for competency could be, 'How serious are you about performance, and the competency framework you have built to bring it about?' A major international energy company is currently using competency assessment as a lever to change previous concepts of performance, and is using pay to support this; the rank order of individuals in a department using competency criteria is quite different from the order that managers would have chosen before, and this is a dramatic way of communicating new values.

Arising from this use of competency assessment is a major pay design issue that needs far greater consideration than can be provided in this chapter. Should competencies be rewarded in base salary, through cash bonuses, or through some other non-cash mechanism? There is as yet no consistent practice in this area as far as the extent to which output-based elements and input-based elements should relate to base salary or cash bonuses. The theoretical case is for competency assessment to drive base salary because it is the sustained area of performance that remains relatively stable over time; whereas time-related objectives are more properly reflected in cash bonuses. However, even in change, conservatism remains, and there seems to be some reluctance as yet for organisations to rely entirely on competency assessment for base salary increases.

SUMMARY

This chapter seeks to provide a framework for understanding the factors that fundamentally determine pay decisions, to examine the notion of competency and to suggest the ways in which competency can best be represented and reflected in pay and pay systems. Many reward strategy and pay structure aspects require detailed consideration in their own right: for instance, criteria for choosing how fixed and variable pay should relate to each other. But here, by concentrating on the structural and causal relationships, we aim to provide the necessary understanding of what is and is not possible. Let us retain core structures founded on the principle of role and organisational requirement; let us express the kinds of competences needed for people to perform their roles in terms which enhance performance and encourage growth; and let us define the underlying competencies that make people successful in particular areas and reward them if they display them.

REFERENCES

1. Murlis, M and Fitt, D 'Job Evaluation in a Changing World' *Personnel Management*, May 1990.
2. 'in our experience': jobs evaluate between 2000 and 4000 Hay job units.
3. Spencer, LM, McClelland, D and Spencer SM (1992) *Competency Assessment Methods: History and State of the Art* Hay/McBer Research Press.

7

Managing Motivation for Performance Improvement

Annick Bernard
Hay Group, France

As managerial styles change, organisations need to look carefully at the business of motivating all their employees. This chapter examines a process for improving managers' performance that is tailored both to the organisation and to the individual.

First we look at the conflicting demands facing today's manager – and in particular human resource and training specialists. How can they introduce sometimes controversial systems of measuring managerial behaviour – the first stage of any improvement programme – in what may be an initially hostile environment?

Next we explain the aims of managing motivation for performance improvement and explore how the process works. The chapter will cover:

- motivation;
- job competency requirements and competencies of the manager;
- managerial styles, with six definitions;
- organisational climate.

MANAGERS IN THE 1990s

What does it mean to manage a team in the 1990s? Managers are constantly flooded with information on who they are, who they should be and above all what outstanding results they should achieve. After obsessively focusing on the threat of Japanese and American competition, executives are now starting to use the 'European threat' on their managers, should they not prove able to match up to the competition. They would be well advised to stop.

Managers are asked to go further and faster and continuously to do better. They are required to motivate their teams and generate results. They are given adequate training to achieve these objectives and they are shown how important it is for them to implement the strategy of the company. However, that strategy is decided by people who all too frequently believe that they do not need to develop their own abilities to lead their people. Managers are then faced with the following paradoxical requirement: they are asked to apply management methods that their own managers often fail to live up to.

The problem arising from the paradox is that pressure to get the best use of the budget means that directors of human resources and heads of training increasingly focus their attention on the return on investment. Companies demand proof from their consultants and trainers: they want to evaluate whether managerial behaviour has been successfully adapted and translated into action. This type of investment cannot always be summed up by a precise cost-benefit analysis. The question can only be answered on a case-by-case basis, by taking into account the specific profile of each organisation.

To do this, consultants may suggest doing an inventory of the company environment. This requires involvement from executives; it means measuring the working climate within the organisation, asking subordinates to evaluate the managerial competencies of their superiors with a simple, precise questionnaire.

The reaction of the organisation to this is immediate and often negative. Despite wanting to increase managerial competencies and to measure the effects of the change, senior executives are not used to the idea of being evaluated by subordinates.

They might instead suggest the use of an evaluation grid that they could use to analyse managerial attitudes over a six-month period. This, however, is not much use if one does not measure progress and if managers cannot get involved in a progress plan stemming from a precise personal evaluation.

The search for a greater coherence between the personality of the manager and the working environment requires information about the impact each has on the other.

Coherence, clarity and consistency may be the stated aims of the company but often executives only pay lip service to them. An approach intended to develop managerial competencies cannot be implemented without an initial diagnosis, nor without a limited, specific and realistic objective. This means:

- an executive board that displays its commitment;
- managers who get involved in a process that takes their environment into account;
- consultants who are professional in the field of training and advising.

Managing a team requires much effort and concentration. Technical expertise is not what makes a difference: behaviour is. Even the most successful managers tend to determine their own behaviour through either a reproduction of or an opposition to the hierarchical model they are given.

This phenomenon is well understood by many directors of human resources and heads of training. Facing various degrees of resistance, they have succeeded in convincing people throughout their entire hierarchical structure to undertake an in-depth reflection on the way in which the company wishes to mobilise its best resources: individual competencies.

THE AIMS OF MANAGING MOTIVATION FOR PERFORMANCE IMPROVEMENT

Managing motivation for performance improvement (MMPI) deals with the use of power and leadership, whatever the culture of the country or the organisation. The process takes into account both individual differences found among managers and collective differences found among organisations.

The objective is simple: to teach managers how to measure the impact of their management on their teams and to modify the way they work if necessary. The resolution of conflicts, the focusing of various individuals on one common goal, the leadership of projects and change require exceptional adaptive and influential skills. For each of these activities both functional and operational management bear the responsibility of managing human resources.

This is why the Hay/McBer approach to management development is based on four key factors which greatly affect the performance of the organisation:

1. individual motivation sources;
2. the requirements of the job;
3. management styles;
4. organisational climate.

We cover these four components of success – or of failure – in turn.

To summarise, an individual joining an organisation with a number of personal motivations is confronted with an environment that will push that person to act and to manage in a way that reconciles his or her personal motives with those of his or her function.

Personal pre-occupations and organisational objectives never coincide perfectly with each other. Any programme intending to develop managerial competencies needs to take this fact into account; otherwise the system is likely to promote management models that are artificial and unconvincing.

The search for a better fit between the person and the environment must never be detrimental to the manager; nor must it be achieved at the expense of the organisation. If flexibility is essential to effective management, it is because of this simple rule of behavioural psychology, repeatedly confirmed by experience: people cannot be ordered to change. The aim of this chapter is to explain the way in which the managing motivation for performance improvement (MMPI) approach helps organisations to cope with the effects of change, to help companies establish the necessary link between the components of the job of the manager and the various priorities of the organisation.

Individual characteristics: motives and competencies

All managers will have noticed the difference between what pushes them to act and what triggers action in a colleague. This acknowledgement is a prerequisite to any change in ways to foster achievement.

The motor of action is each individual's social motivation. Associated with every manager's culture, education, training and know-how, this social motivation underlies all their competencies, whatever their stage of development. Hay/McBer has developed a method that enables organisations to decode internal motivation based on the research carried out by David McClelland[1].

Three social motives

Three social motives can be determined and evaluated for each individual that condition that individual's behaviours and competencies. The combination of the drive for achievement, the desire to maintain friendly relationships with others and the power drive, or desire to be influential over, one's environment result in different professional attitudes, depending on the degree of intensity of each.

By imagining a number of thoughts and acts in specific situations, which are then screened through a precise decoding method, the process results in a personal motivation profile. The main characteristics of the profile attached to each dominant motivation are as follows. The *drive for achievement* expresses itself through:

- a tendency to take reasonable risks;
- the desire to take sole responsibility for results, that is, not to be involved in processes in which chance has an important role to play;
- the need to know quickly whether one's work was correctly done or not;
- a permanent concern for personal improvement;
- a genuine interest in innovation and efficiency (how to do things better, faster, differently).

Many managers believe that they fall into this category simply because of the fact that in the culture of our industrial corporations, performance is the key value. However, the cultural atmosphere needs to be disassociated for actual behaviours. Superior performance can be achieved for motives other than a high achievement drive. These motives are internal, that is deep-rooted and not necessarily detectable at first glance.

Certain people are more concerned than others with the need to establish, maintain or re-establish *friendly relationships* with others. This need results in:

- a greater receptivity to factors affecting relationships at work;
- the ability to establish and to maintain convivial and friendly relationships;
- the fear of losing these relationships.

The will to influence

The word power often has negative connotations in our European culture. This term seems solidly linked to the idea of coercion of others, and calls political power to mind, which is no longer highly regarded. But in terms of competencies, *the will to influence* and to be powerful manifests itself through:

- the desire to impress others through action or through words;
- attempts to influence others to improve one's prestige (personal power) or for the common good (socialised power);
- concern for one's reputation;
- a capacity spontaneously to offer support and advice.

The need for definitions of personal motives is because managers who have a strong achievement drive do not lead their teams in the same way as those who are highly motivated by an affiliation need or by a power drive.

Personal motives orient and direct professional behaviour. They translate into strong and weak points in terms of competencies. If a person fears other people's reactions but has the will to influence, that person will not use her or his competencies in the same way as a colleague facing the same professional environment with no fear of rejection and a strong focus on his or her field.

If someone's primary objective in life, which may be subconscious but is always personal, is to establish friendly relations with others, all efforts will instinctively be directed towards the achievement of that goal. A power or an achievement drive may also motivate that person but to a lesser extent. The competencies put to use at work will be greater in those fields in which someone instinctively feels at ease.

Figure 7.1 illustrates the personal motivation profile of the head of a department in a large structure. Further on in this chapter we will see how the competencies that this person demonstrates when carrying out his job are linked to his sources of motivation.

These are only a few examples of competencies necessary for successful management. During the MMPI programme, consultants and participants scrutinise 20 main competencies that are detailed in the chapter 'Selection and recruitment'.

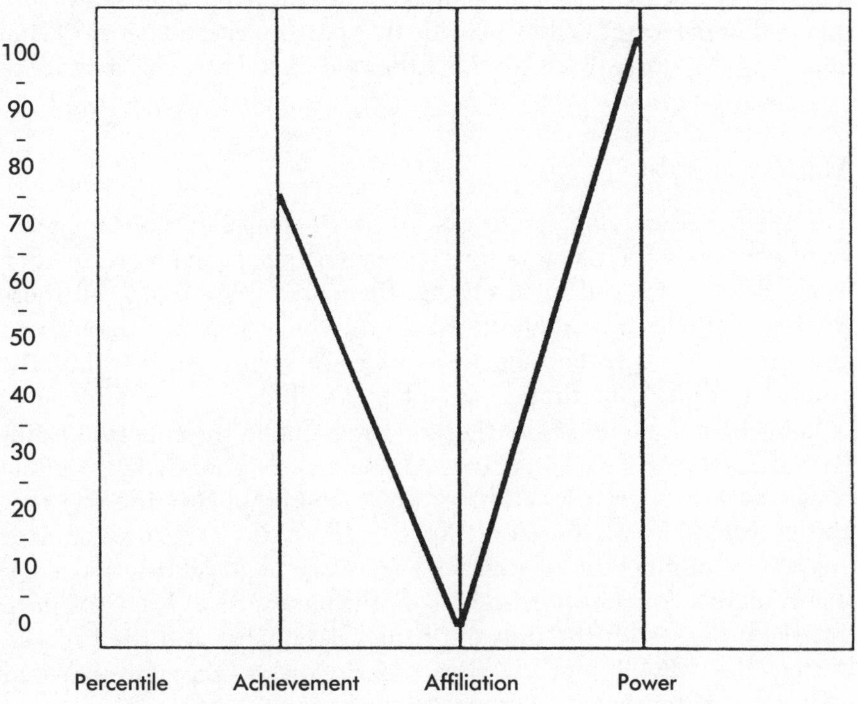

Figure 7.1 Personal motivation profile – department head

JOB COMPETENCY REQUIREMENTS: THE MANAGER

The competency requirements of the role that the manager occupies are determined using the methodology described in detail in earlier chapters – particularly the chapter on selection and recruitment. The goal of the process is to identify those competencies that are crucial to the performance of the team.

Naturally, these competencies vary from field to field and from job to job, and are accordingly selected and adapted to the case at hand in the process of applying the MMPI method.

The basic principle remains the same: Hay/McBer tutors submit to each manager her or his motivational profile as well as a diagnosis of her or his competencies. They then work together with managers to determine what they need to improve, given the accountabilities of their jobs. Once this work is completed, efforts focus on the way in which she or he manages the team: how does the manager work with this or that person? Do they provide that person with guidance? What impact do they have on results? In other words, what is this manager's management style?

Managerial styles

There is a considerable amount of literature available about management styles and their adaptations to various European environments, from Blake and Mouton to Hersey-Blanchard. Essentially, all these works boil down to an analysis of how A, who is in power, goes about 'bringing B to do something he would not have done without the intervention of A', (definition of Robert Dahl).

In his book *La société bloquée* (Editions de Seuil) in the chapter dealing with the issue of power in advanced societies, Michel Crozler defines power both as 'a relation and a process', and highlights the fact that 'the power relation is not only specific; it is also reciprocal'. Power involves a number of negotiations between supervisors and their subordinates. For that precise reason, the approach of Hay/McBer in this field focuses on the impact of the relationship and the process. Within the MMPI method, the description of the six styles of management focuses on the various role components which constitute 'management':

- listen;
- determine objectives and targets against which to measure performance;
- elaborate action plans and lead projects;
- give direction to the team;
- inform everyone about his or her work;
- evaluate results;
- provide co-workers with growth opportunities;
- establish interpersonal relationships.

This short list of managers' roles could be increased, just as eight or ten management styles could be identified instead of six. But the methodology is less important than the way in which we use it, because it is the basis of exchanges between a manager and his team, or among managers of the same hierarchical level.

In other words, the relevance of the description suggested by Hay/McBer of these management styles on the quality of the analysis of the accountabilities of the job and of the profile of the manager, and of their co-workers as well.

Modern managers may scoff at the idea that a good manager must adapt their management style to each of their co-workers. It means that the manager is required to identify with each member of the team while meeting the targets set, preserving a positive working climate and implementing the strategy decided by the Board.

The purpose of a diagnosis of styles of management consists of identifying nuances and modulations in the way in which A influences B, with or without hierarchical power. Below we provide a brief outline of the different management styles.

Coercive style
The general attitude of this style may be summed up as 'Do as I say!'

Typical behaviours:

- Gives clear directives – or orders – and does not take preferences of co-workers into account;

- closely controls, appreciates detailed reporting;
- aims at absolute mastery of operations;
- tends to make negative evaluations;
- threatens to impose sanctions to put pressure on co-workers to achieve results.

When does this style prove effective?

- To manage crisis and emergency situations;
- when small deviations from norms are likely to create severe problems;

When does this style prove ineffective?

- In the long term; fosters passivity, rebellion, and various avoidance behaviours;
- with co-workers from whom initiative and innovative capacity is required.

Very few managers think that they adopt this style, and that is mostly the case. However, one can manage extremely authoritatively, but in a subtle, tactful way. Co-workers are rarely mistaken about this point; their perception is therefore crucial to the validity of the outcome of the method.

Authoritative style
The general attitude of this style is, 'I'm firm but fair'.

Typical behaviours:

- Gives clear directives in a tactful manner;
- takes most decisions on their own;
- listens to the ideas and opinions of co-workers;
- exposes the reasons for decisions as well as the purpose of the directives that they communicate;
- influences by pinpointing to co-workers where their interest lies as well as that of the organisation;

- supervises the work without over attention to details;
- has the ability to give positive as well as negative evaluations.

When does this style prove effective?

- When the job requires precise directives and targets (which is often the case);
- when the manager is well accepted by their co-workers, and when their expertise is recognised in the organisation.

When does this style prove ineffective?

- When the manager forgets to foster growth among co-workers, which tends to limit initiative;
- when the expertise of the manager is questioned in the organisation.

Affiliative style

The general attitude of this style is, 'All will go well as long as I preserve a good working climate'.

Typical behaviours:

- Does not strive to give clear and precise directives;
- gets interested in material and psychological working conditions to ensure the well-being of co-workers;
- avoids conflicts as much as possible;
- tends to rely on individual characteristics to evaluate co-workers rather than on actual results;
- strives to be and remain popular;
- has difficulties in giving a negative evaluation.

When does this style prove effective?

- When business is relatively easy and co-workers master their jobs well;
- when one-off, personal help is needed;

- when co-ordination of people and of teams is needed;
- in an environment in which a good working climate is essential.

When does this style prove ineffective?

- When co-workers come up with poor results;
- when a crisis or an emergency situation requires precise directives (our experience proves that the affiliative style often turns into a coercive one when difficulties arise, because of the manager's fear of being unable to master the situation).

Democratic style
The general attitude of this style is, 'I'll listen to your opinions and I take them into account'.

Typical behaviours:

- Leads the team through empowerment of co-workers;
- involves co-workers in decision-making;
- prefers to rely on consensus-building;
- organises participative meetings;
- expects attainment of targets, but does not constantly ask for more;
- gives negative evaluations in extreme situations only.

When does this style prove effective?

- When the team is competent and shares information with the manager;
- when the job requires extensive co-ordination.

When does this style prove ineffective?

- When meetings are not an option;
- when the work of the co-workers requires close control.

Pace-setting style
The general attitude of this style is, 'Do as I say and all will go well'.

Typical behaviours:

- Leads by means of the example they embody;
- sets high targets corresponding to personal criteria;
- has difficulties delegating because of the feeling that they can do better than the co-workers;
- has difficulties accepting standard or insufficient results, which foster coercion and recourse to sanctions;
- does not provide much growth opportunity to co-workers;
- prefers to take the responsibilities alone rather than to lead the team.

When does this style prove effective?

- When co-workers are extremely motivated and competent and do not need to be co-ordinated too much;
- when experts or individual contributions must be managed.

When does this style prove ineffective?

- When the manager depends on the work of co-workers and the job requires extensive delegation;
- when the teamwork spirit and co-workers' personal growth prove indispensable.

Coaching style
The general attitude of this style is, 'I am sure you can succeed'.

Typical behaviours:

- Actively helps co-workers and shows them how to improve their results;
- looks for opportunities to develop co-workers and help them grow;
- encourages co-workers to set their own goals and targets and to establish their action plans;

- investigates how to make the best use of the competencies of each co-worker.

When does this method prove effective?

- When the manager displays performance measurement variables and evaluates target-meeting of co-workers;
- when the team is determined, takes initiative and is ready to move on professionally.

When does this method prove ineffective?

- When the manager's expertise is insufficient;
- when co-workers are not competent enough and need strong direction.

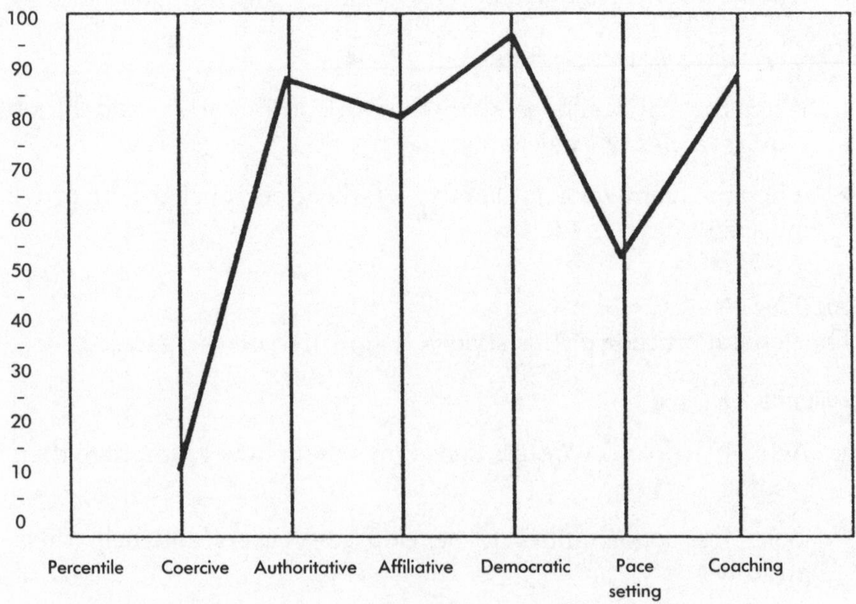

Figure 7.2 Management style inventory – participant response

Personal motivation and management styles

The link now needs to be established between management styles and motivation. Let us return to the example given in Figure 7.1. What is the dominant management style of this manager, who, as we now know, is strongly motivated by achievement and power? The answers he gave in the diagnosis of management styles differ from those of his co-workers.

The perception gap is considerable. The manager sees himself as authoritative, affiliative, democratic and coaching (see Figure 7.2), whereas his co-workers see him as authoritative, pace-setting and democratic (see Figure 7.3). Their perception, however, would fit the motivation profile of the manager (achievement and power).

The gaps between the results of the team and that of its leader were looked at carefully. As the team was highly competent, the possibility was investigated of developing further the coaching style within the

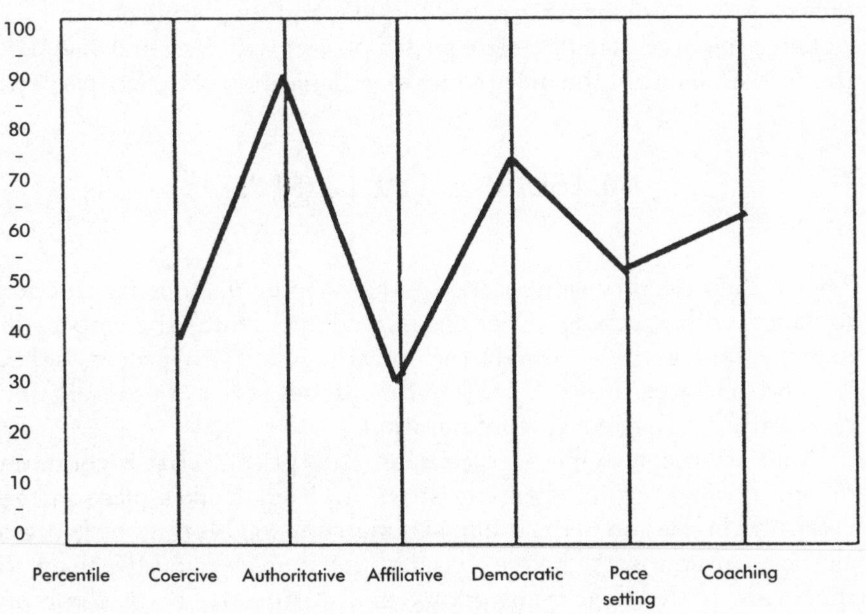

Figure 7.3 Management style inventory – subordinates response

job, which entailed evolution of jobs, new responsibilities, etc. Finally, the head of department and his team members elaborated a change project that focused on:

- the delegation of certain responsibilities such as the representation of the team outside the organisation;
- the development of the activities of certain jobs held by team members;
- the management of communication with another unit in the organisation;
- training for two of the co-workers;
- a modification of the targets of the project.

The team members took part in the improvement of their own competencies. This simple example illustrates the type of work that can be carried out with the Hay/McBer method. The goal is not to please the manager or his co-workers, but to improve the fit between the team, ie the manager and co-workers, and their environment.

Thus, the need is to complete such a project with a shared vision of the work unit and of the more complex organisation of which it is part.

MEASURING THE CLIMATE

Throughout the process described in this chapter, diagnostics are used together with teaching experiences to demonstrate the impact of management on the team. What is innovative about this process is that its approach integrates a dimension that proves both ever-present and constantly overlooked: the organisation.

What are the systems in place in an enterprise? What is common practice? What are its characteristics? And what takes place in the work unit in relation to the organisational context? During the process all these questions will be answered by the manager and the team so they can share their perceptions and formulate their common objectives.

Motivations underlie behaviours and competencies as well as

management styles. Competencies and management styles have an impact on people and on structures. These structures affect people and change them as well. Hay/McBer uses six components to demonstrate the climate of the organisation when investigating the 'atmosphere' that reigns in a given enterprise. The definitions of these six components are listed below. As imperfect as they may be, these components were thought out to measure the impact of procedures and of processes. What is described by the people who fill in the questionnaire is not necessarily an accurate and complete picture of reality; nor is it meant that way. It simply reflects what these people perceive in the workplace.

1. *Flexibility:* Are the procedures and formalities perceived as useful and necessary to the accomplishment of work? Are people encouraged to develop new ideas and approaches?
2. *Responsibility:* Is it accepted that members of the organisation feel free to take decisions on their own about the way they go about their work? To what extent are they encouraged to take risks?
3. *Standards:* How demanding and ambitious are the performance criteria and objectives determined by management? To what extent do people feel stimulated to improve their performance?
4. *Reward:* How strong is the link between reward and performance, and to what extent is it perceived as strong? Do messages of positive feedback exceed threats and criticisms?
5. *Clarity:* Is the strategy, the global project for the department or the work unit, clear to all? Does the co-worker know what is expected of him or her?
6. *Commitment and team spirit:* To what extent are the members of the organisation ready to make an extra effort when it proves necessary? How proud do the members feel about belonging to their work unit or to the organisation?

In large organisations, the climate measured will be that of the structure in which the work unit under consideration operates, not that of the entire organisation. The measuring of the climate of an organisation enables evaluation both of the climate as is and the climate that the members of the team would like to see.

As for the head of a department in a large structure and his team referred to earlier, the working climate in his department changed. He had a more positive view of the organisation than his team, and had rated responsibility and clarity higher than they did. As a result, a number of requests for clarification arose concerning the development of the structure and its relative positioning in the global strategy of the organisation.

The manager and his team set up an action plan in the improvement areas identified in the course of the MMPI process. The various diagnostics that initiate the process of change fostered by the MMPI translate into training and the supervision of action plans in the workplace. The heavy involvement of people in the process is secured by guarantees of confidentiality, and by the partnership as the very basis of the contract between the enterprise and the consultants.

Case study

Michael Robidoux had had a highly successful five years with a major financial services group, building a regional business from scratch. From the tentative beginnings of a product appreciation course, a desk and a telephone, he had been able to build a substantial client base both in corporate and individual business. Through three area managers he now manages a group of 23 people.

Although growth had been healthy and targets met, Michael was becoming increasingly concerned about whether he could sustain success and growth. He himself was still bringing in some 30 per cent of the corporate business (and nearly half the new business). He was attracting good quality people but the best of them were tending to leave after 18 months, just when they were becoming really effective; and the general climate did not seem very positive.

In our experience, Michael is not untypical of many thousands of managers. They find that available management development programmes are not integrated in their approach; they do not understand clearly how they should behave in particular situations to achieve the best results; and although they can spot several clues they have no model in their minds which links the course of these elements and provides a framework for behaving in a way that leads to positive changes.

Michael attended the programme and understood why the high achievement drive and impatience with poor standards that had been the basis of his own success translated into a pace-setting management style. This created a climate in which his subordinates felt they had little responsibility, were infrequently and inconsistently recognised, and eventually they inevitably became frustrated.

Michael experimented on the programme with more appropriate democratic and coaching styles; and he planned for a permanent change by setting himself objectives to control natural strengths, develop weaker competencies, and introduce new management practices. For example, on his return, he introduced performance planning and review processes in his region because, for the first time, he saw that they were important management processes rather than procedures imposed by head office. His best sales people are staying; and in a difficult market place, signs of growth are returning.

SUMMARY

The era of stress and of pressure is outdated: Japanese are increasingly taking vacations, and European managers will be attracted to those companies that do not pressure them to increase their motivation or competitivity. In our collective memory, profiles of heroes are beginning to change. The model of the well-balanced manager who works fairly and adapts behaviours to objectives is replacing that of the short-term performance-obsessed manager. Companies need to understand this evolution if they are to retain their most valuable managers. Managers will wish to rediscover the pleasure of working in a relaxed atmosphere.

Plurality of management styles, team flexibility, realism of objectives: all these simple values need to underline the company's operations if managers are to be given an environment in which they are stimulated to manage properly. When the supervisory role fosters too great a tension and too many internal conflicts, the leading of a team becomes a burden rather than a challenge for the manager.

Companies wishing to progress need to start consistently developing the managerial competencies of its managers. Such competencies rarely develop in the midst of demotivation and discouragement.

The aim of this chapter was to clarify the close links between the requirements of a job, individual competencies, management styles and the climate of the organisation. Good or bad management styles do not exist. In reality, management styles are more or less adapted to a given context, just as the choice of some critical fields of competence is at the root of the success of a given organisation.

To understand the underlying motivations of people, to select and train managers and teams on the basis of the relevant competencies, to develop realistic action plans while taking all these elements into account: these are powerful means to create the best collective performance of a team, a department, and to contribute to the overall performance of the enterprise.

REFERENCES

1. McClelland, D (1987) *Human Motivation*, Cambridge University Press.

Index

Index

Index

Index

Index